HIDEKI ENDO
AYOUNG CHANG MAKOTO ISHII
KAZUNARI NAKAMURA IAN KITTICHAI
NICOLAS CHANG WUTTISAK WUTTHAMPORN
VICKY LAU JEREMIAH STONE
ATSUSHI UCHIBORI LANSHU CHEN
SUN KIM BYOUNG-JIN KIM AKIRA SUGIURA
DHARSHAN MUNIDASA PANG KOK KEONG RYUJI TESHIMA
BERNHART DENNY SUMARKO HAJIME YONEDA
AKIRA BACK BONGSU KIM JOWETT YU
ZOR TAN CHEONG THIN SHOTA NAKAJIMA BANG KI SU JIMMY LIM

CHEFS

DAN HONG KAI HO
ASAI MASASHI
SURAKIT KHEMKAEW
RENU HOMSOMBAT
COLLECTIVE
DAK LADDAPORN WICHANGOEN KENICHI YAMAMOTO PETER SERPICO
KEI KOBAYASHI XAVIER HSU SAM LEONG
ALAIN HUANG TAE HWAN RYU TONY YOO
EUNJUNG CHO MARGARITA FORÉS
DAUNGPORN SONGVISAVA TAKU SEKINE
YOON HWAYOUNG HIDEAKI SATO
TAMMY MAH KAZUYA SUGIURA
HIROYASU KAWATE
SEUNG HWAN CARLOS SHIN

Michelle Tchea

HIDEKI ENDO
MAKOTO ISHII
AYOUNG CHANG
KAZUNARI NAKAMURA IAN KITTICHAI
NICOLAS CHANG WUTTISAK WUTHAMPORN
VICKY LAU JEREMIAH STONE
ATSUSHI UCHIBORI **LANSHU CHEN**
SUN KIM BYOUNG-JIN KIM AKIRA SUGIURA
DHARSHAN MUNIDASA PANG KOK KEONG RYUJI TESHIMA
BERNHART DENNY SUMARKO **HAJIME YONEDA**
AKIRA BACK BONGSU KIM JOWETT YU
ZOR TAN CHEONG THIN SHOTA NAKAJIMA BANG KI SU JIMMY LIM

CHEFS

COLLECTIVE

DAN HONG KAI HO
ASAI MASASHI
SURAKIT KHEMKAEW
RENU HOMSOMBAT
DAK LADDAPORN WICHANGOEN KENICHI YAMAMOTO PETER SERPICO
KEI KOBAYASHI XAVIER HSU SAM LEONG
ALAIN HUANG TAE HWAN RYU TONY YOO
EUNJUNG CHO **MARGARITA FORÉS**
DAUNGPORN SONGVISAVA TAKU SEKINE
YOON HWAYOUNG **HIDEAKI SATO**
TAMMY MAH KAZUYA SUGIURA
HIROYASU KAWATE
SEUNG HWAN CARLOS SHIN

RECIPES, TIPS & SECRETS FROM 50 OF THE WORLD'S GREATEST CHEFS

Marshall Cavendish
Cuisine

Editor: Melissa Tham
Designer: Bernard Go Kwang Meng

© 2017 Marshall Cavendish International (Asia) Private Limited
Text and recipes © Michelle Tchea

All images courtesy of the respective restaurants except
page 18: Chef's portrait by Jamie K. Morton
page 34: Chef's portrait by Honshu Wang
pages 78–79: Chef's portrait and image of dish by LisaKleinMichel
page 65: Image of dish by Frame Photographics
pages 98–99: Chef's portrait and image of dish by Suzi Pratt
pages 120–121: Chef's portrait and image of dish by Tammy Mah
page 122: Author's photo by Sacha Bosman

Published by Marshall Cavendish Cuisine
An imprint of Marshall Cavendish International

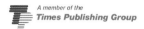

A member of the
Times Publishing Group

Other Marshall Cavendish Offices:
Marshall Cavendish Corporation. 99 White Plains Road, Tarrytown NY 10591-9001, USA
• Marshall Cavendish International (Thailand) Co Ltd. 253 Asoke, 12th Flr,
Sukhumvit 21 Road, Klongtoey Nua, Wattana, Bangkok 10110, Thailand •
Marshall Cavendish (Malaysia) Sdn Bhd, Times Subang, Lot 46, Subang Hi-Tech Industrial
Park, Batu Tiga, 40000 Shah Alam, Selangor Darul Ehsan, Malaysia

Marshall Cavendish is a registered trademark of Times Publishing Limited

National Library Board, Singapore Cataloguing-in-Publication Data

Name(s): Tchea, Michelle. | Tham, Melissa, editor. | Go, Kwang Meng, designer.
Title: Chefs collective : recipes, tips & secrets from 50 of the world's greatest chefs /
Michelle Tchea ; editor, Melissa Tham ; designer, Bernard Go Kwang Meng.
Description: Singapore : Marshall Cavendish Cuisine, [2017]
Identifier(s): OCN 972698575 | ISBN 978-981-47-7192-4 (hardcover)
Subject(s): LCSH: Cookbooks. | Cooking, Asian. | Cooking, American | Cooking, European.
Classification: DDC 641.59 -- dc23

Printed by Times Offset (M) Sdn Bhd

For Dad and Mum.

An amuse-bouche to whet the appetite.

Thanks for always being hungry.

CONTENTS

ACKNOWLEDGEMENTS

The words *oui, ye,* 好, *ja* were music to my ears when planning this book.

Thank you to all the wonderful chefs who answered my emails, responded to my phone messages and entertained my visits to their restaurants. *Chefs Collective* is only possible with your wonderful support, dedication and words of encouragement. I'm truly privileged and immensely grateful for your support.

To my publisher, Marshall Cavendish, and the team behind *Chefs Collective,* Lydia and Melissa – thank you for always emailing back, listening to my crazy ideas and of course, making *Chefs Collective* a reality.

To my family – another one!

To my friends – this is the fourth time you have supported me (and it might not be the last!).

PREFACE

Have you heard about the new chefs in Taiwan serving some of the best French food outside of France? What about the brigade of Japanese chefs in Paris, revolutionising and changing the way Parisians eat? And did you know that some of the world's most highly awarded chefs are in fact female and come from the Philippines, Thailand and Taiwan?

In the heart of bustling Taipei, a chef stands in his kitchen, awaiting yet another steady stream of diners to enter his restaurant. Having worked with celebrity chefs in Europe, the young talent is stepping out of their shadow and turning heads with his bistronomy-style cuisine. Focusing on native Taiwanese ingredients with creative flair and modern appeal, the chef now has a legion of young apprentice chefs who look upon his achievements in awe.

In the Charles de Gaulle-Étoile neighbourhood of Paris, a Japanese-born chef is getting ready for another packed house for dinner. The chic, gastronomic restaurant fits perfectly with the high fashion district of the Champs-Élysées with items like smoked bonito over hay with a cream of lemon confit. The *cromesquis* of foie gras and monkfish from Noirmoutier in a shellfish with green yuzu sauce is not typically Japanese nor is it French bistro-style, but it is one of the hottest dishes in Paris.

In 'restaurant-dense' Copenhagen, Denmark, a young chef pays tribute to the flavours and techniques of her home country, Thailand. Fuelled by curiosity and determination to educate diners on flavours not readily seen as 'gourmet' in this Scandinavian country, this young female chef has slowly won the love and affection of the Danes, with dishes like fried foie gras served with ginger and plum wine, as well as grilled baby squid topped with home-made chicken sausage and aromatics, reminding guests of a Thai street market... but better.

Daring, innovative and highly ambitious, these award-winning chefs in *Chefs Collective,* are the epitome of hardworking, passionate and bona fide talents in the kitchen.

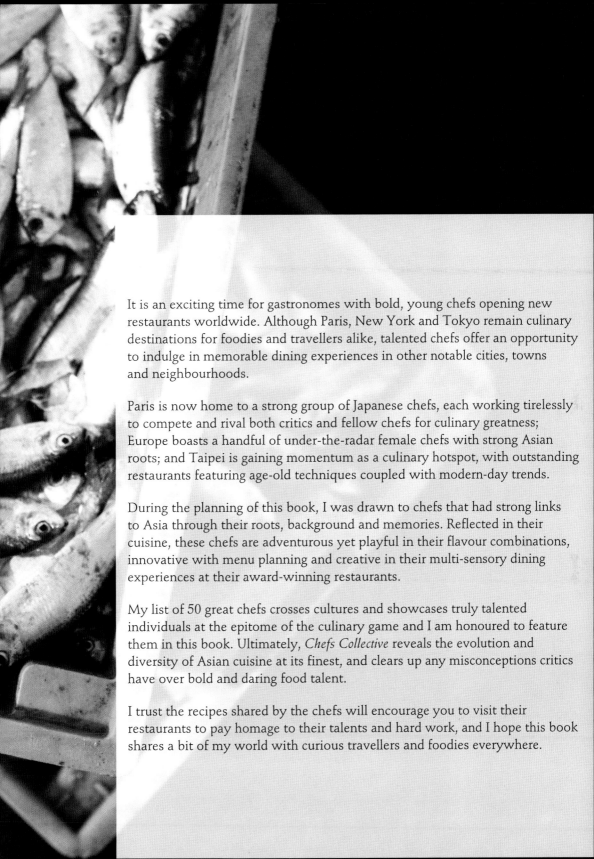

It is an exciting time for gastronomes with bold, young chefs opening new restaurants worldwide. Although Paris, New York and Tokyo remain culinary destinations for foodies and travellers alike, talented chefs offer an opportunity to indulge in memorable dining experiences in other notable cities, towns and neighbourhoods.

Paris is now home to a strong group of Japanese chefs, each working tirelessly to compete and rival both critics and fellow chefs for culinary greatness; Europe boasts a handful of under-the-radar female chefs with strong Asian roots; and Taipei is gaining momentum as a culinary hotspot, with outstanding restaurants featuring age-old techniques coupled with modern-day trends.

During the planning of this book, I was drawn to chefs that had strong links to Asia through their roots, background and memories. Reflected in their cuisine, these chefs are adventurous yet playful in their flavour combinations, innovative with menu planning and creative in their multi-sensory dining experiences at their award-winning restaurants.

My list of 50 great chefs crosses cultures and showcases truly talented individuals at the epitome of the culinary game and I am honoured to feature them in this book. Ultimately, *Chefs Collective* reveals the evolution and diversity of Asian cuisine at its finest, and clears up any misconceptions critics have over bold and daring food talent.

I trust the recipes shared by the chefs will encourage you to visit their restaurants to pay homage to their talents and hard work, and I hope this book shares a bit of my world with curious travellers and foodies everywhere.

Alain Huang
QUAIL WITH LEEK AND BARLEY | 14

Asai Masashi
BEEF TONGUE | 16

Ayoung Chang
BEEF CARPACCIO AND DRIED SEAWEED WITH GLUTINOUS RICE | 18

Bernhart Denny Sumarko
LAMB SATAY | 20

Bongsu Kim
PIG'S HEAD PYEONYUK | 22

Dan Hong
VIETNAMESE STEAK TARTARE | 24

Daungporn Songvisava
GREEN CURRY WITH CHICKEN | 26

Hajime Yoneda
SORA | 28

Jimmy Lim Tyan Yaw
BAK KUT TEH | 30

Jowett Yu
MUM'S 'MOSTLY CABBAGE, A LITTLE BIT OF PORK' DUMPLINGS | 32

Kai Ho
65°C EGG, YILAN 'YA SHANG' WITH TARO,
SAKURA SHRIMP AND CRISPY SHALLOTS | 34

Kenichi Yamamoto
BOUDIN NOIR WITH PARSLEY BREADCRUMBS | 36

Ryuji Teshima
SLOW-COOKED CHICKEN WITH POACHED EGG AND WHITE WINE SAUCE | 38

Sam Leong
DOUBLE-BOILED MILKY CHICKEN BROTH WITH MOREL MUSHROOM AND
WILD BAMBOO PITH IN WHOLE FRAGRANT COCONUT | 40

Tony Yoo Hyun Su
JEJU BLACK PIG SSAM WITH WILD MUSHROOM AND
FERMENTED SOYBEAN PASTE | 42

Xavier Hsu
PORK BELLY | 44

Yoon Hwayoung
LAMB WITH KOREAN CHIVES | 46

ALAIN HUANG

Executive Chef, RAW

Taipei, Taiwan

French cuisine

Cooking style
Ideas inspired from memory and presented spontaneously into reality.

Background story behind this dish
At RAW, we often use modern Western techniques with Taiwanese ingredients to redefine traditional Taiwanese flavours. This dish pays homage to my Taiwanese roots as it combines Western ingredients such as barley risotto and quail with soy crumbs, an ingredient that is very commonly used in Taiwan.

Cooking philosophy
Zero waste. I try to use every part of the ingredient to the best of my abilities.

Biggest achievement
I don't dwell on my past achievements because I believe there will always be room for improvement, and it has become my motivation to be better than who I was.

Earliest memory with food
First dumpling that I made by myself. It was the first time I cooked for my family, and my parents were really proud of me.

Quail with Leek and Barley

Serves 2–4

2 quails

30 g (1 oz) honey

100 ml (3^1/$_2$ fl oz / ^{2}/$_5$ cup) light soy sauce

2 leeks

100 g (3^1/$_2$ oz) soy crumbs

75 g (2^3/$_5$ oz) butter

300 g (11 oz) barley

500 g (1 lb 1^1/$_2$ oz) baby spinach, blanched

200 ml (6^3/$_4$ fl oz / ^{4}/$_5$ cup) chicken stock

Oil as needed

Salt to taste

Ground white pepper to taste

GARNISH
5 silver onions, peeled and sliced into rings

METHOD

Marinate quails with honey and light soy sauce. Set aside for 2 hours.

Drain quails and air-dry in fridge for another 2 hours.

Preheat oven to 230°C (450°F). Roast leeks until soft and tender. Set aside.

Toast soy crumbs in a pan until golden brown. Add butter and cook until fragrant.

Boil barley in lightly salted water until soft.

Place blanched spinach and chicken stock in a food processor and process into a smooth purée. Mix barley with spinach purée.

Preheat oven to 180°C (350°F). Heat sufficient oil for deep-frying in a pan until 185°C (365°F) and deep-fry quails for 2 minutes. Drain and place in oven for 1 minute. Set aside to rest for 1 minute before seasoning with salt and pepper. Cut quails into half.

Serve quail with barley and spinach purée, leeks and soy crumbs. Garnish with onion rings.

ASAI MASASHI

Chef, BINCHO

Singapore

Modern Yakitori cuisine

Cooking style
Yakitori.

Biggest achievement
A few Michelin-starred chefs visited Bincho and really liked our food. They gave very positive feedback on the dishes and this made me very happy.

Motivation to becoming a chef
I've always liked experimenting with food and through that, I discovered my passion for cooking.

Best thing about being a chef
The best thing about being a chef is seeing your diners happy and satisfied after their meals. As a chef, that is what keeps me going.

Worst thing about being a chef
It is very challenging to hire suitable kitchen staff these days.

Cooking tips
Always take feedback positively and constantly work on improving my dishes.

Beef Tongue

Serves 4

BEEF TONGUE

1¹/₂–2 kg (4 lb 6 oz) beef tongue

10 g (¹/₃ oz) English parsley stems

2 medium carrots, peeled and sliced

2 radish stems

Salt as needed

Ground black pepper as needed

Shoyu (Japanese soy sauce) as needed

GARLIC BUTTER

250 g (9 oz) unsalted butter

20 g (²/₃ oz) salt

150 g (5¹/₃ oz) garlic, peeled and chopped

10 g (¹/₃ oz) English parsley, peeled and chopped

METHOD

Prepare beef tongue 1 day ahead. Place beef tongue, English parsley stems, carrots and radish stems in a pressure cooker and cook for about 45 minutes.

Remove beef tongue and gently peel off skin while still warm. Let beef tongue cool before placing in the chiller overnight.

Prepare garlic butter. Mix butter, salt, garlic and English parsley in a large bowl. Place bowl in chiller until ready to use.

Season chilled beef tongue with some salt and pepper. Grill until beef tongue is seared on both sides. Brush grilled beef tongue with shoyu, followed by garlic butter. Return to oven and grill for another 5–6 minutes until garlic butter is lightly brown.

Slice, garnish as desired and serve.

AYOUNG CHANG

Chef at JIA, BEAU RIVAGE

Mississippi, USA

Asian Fusion cuisine

Cooking style
Asian fusion. Fermented food.

Background story behind this dish
This dish is very popular in Korea. It also
perfectly complements my cooking style
of using fermented foods in a fusion way.

What is your favourite food city
Bangkok. I love that they have diverse
ingredients that when combined, make
well-balanced dishes with many health
benefits.

Kitchen utensils you can't live without
I couldn't go without a good sharp knife,
measuring cups and spoons.

Best thing about being a chef
There is never a dull day in the life of a
chef. Sometimes I will think about a menu
or a dish at night and I can't wait to test it
out the next day.

Worst thing about being a chef
The worst thing about being a chef is you
have to be almost 100% dedicated to the
kitchen and that doesn't leave much time
for my family.

Beef Carpaccio and Dried Seaweed with Glutinous Rice

Serves 2–4

1 egg yolk

$^1/_2$ Tbsp light soy sauce

$^1/_2$ Korean pear, peeled and
cut into thin strips

1 tsp black sesame seeds

1 tsp roasted pine nuts

BEEF CARPACCIO

200 g (7 oz) wagyu beef

Salt to taste

Sugar to taste

Garlic to taste

Sesame oil to taste

DRIED SEAWEED WITH GLUTINOUS RICE

185 g (6$^1/_2$ oz) glutinous rice

750 ml (24 fl oz / 3 cups)
dashi broth

Nori (seaweed) as needed, wiped
clean with a damp towel

1 Tbsp salt

$^1/_2$ tsp dried shrimp powder

Sesame seeds as needed

Oil as needed

METHOD

Prepare glutinous rice for dried seaweed with glutinous rice 2 weeks ahead. Leave glutinous rice to ferment in cold water for 2 weeks.

Drain and grind fermented glutinous rice. Cook in dashi broth until a thick porridge is acquired. Allow to cool at room temperature.

Layer 2 sheets of *nori* together on a bamboo sushi mat and brush with glutinous rice porridge. Sprinkle with salt, dried shrimp powder and sesame seeds. Repeat until glutinous rice porridge is used up.

Place *nori* in a dehydrator at 51.6°C (125°F) for 20 hours until hard and firm. Alternatively, let *nori* dry naturally on bamboo mats for about 1 week. Prepare sufficient oil for deep-frying and deep-fry *nori* until crisp. Set aside to drain. Break into chips.

Prepare beef carpaccio. Season beef with salt, sugar, garlic and sesame oil. Slice beef very thinly.

To serve, place egg yolk in a bowl with soy sauce and serve as a dipping sauce. Wrap a few strips of pear in beef. Dip edges of beef in black sesame seeds. Top with pine nuts. Serve beef carpaccio with dried seaweed with glutinous rice.

BERNHART DENNY SUMARKO

Chef de Cuisine,
BLANCO PAR MANDIF

Ubud, Bali, Indonesia

Progressive Indonesian
cuisine

Cooking style
Progressive Asian.

Background story behind this dish
Satay usually refers to anything you put on a skewer, be it chicken, beef or lamb. We smother it with a combination of crushed peanuts, sweet soy sauce and a bit of chilli. It's served at many stalls in Indonesia and every region has their take on it, but the core remains the same: protein on a skewer with a sweet soy sauce/peanut/chilli combo. The idea came when I was sitting under a tree, eating satay with the guys after a work shift (as usual) and one of them joked "if only we can do something this good and this simple at the restaurant". We decided to give this recipe a little twist by presenting the lamb satay without the skewers.

Cooking philosophy
Always empty your glass before interacting with someone else. That way, they'll fill you up with their knowledge and experience.

Cooking tips
Invest in a good knife and a good attitude, and everything will be revealed to you at a certain pace. No rush.

Lamb Satay

Serves 2–4

1 rack of lamb

Sea salt to taste

Freshly cracked black pepper to taste

1 tsp sunflower oil

1 clove garlic, peeled

1 stalk lemongrass, smashed

2 g kaffir lime leaves

Roughly chopped peanuts as needed

Fried shallots as needed

SATAY GLAZE

30 g (1 oz) Japanese miso

1 tsp sweet soy sauce

PEANUT SAUCE

50 g (1³/₄ oz) peanuts

150 g (5¹/₃ oz) cashews

2 cloves garlic, peeled

2 shallots, peeled

5 g (¹/₆ oz) *kaferia* galangal

2 g kaffir lime leaves

20 g (²/₃ oz) red chillies, seeded

5 g (¹/₆ oz) bird's eye chillies

5 g (¹/₆ oz) candlenuts

Salt to taste

Sugar to taste

5 g (¹/₆ oz) brown sugar

TIP
Toast the nuts well to get a delicious nutty flavour from the peanut sauce. Choose the best sweet soy sauce you can get!

METHOD

Clean and slice lamb rack into individual lamb pieces. Trim all sinews and remove excess fat. Season lamb with salt and pepper.

Prepare satay glaze. Combine ingredients in a bowl and mix well. Set aside.

Preheat oven to 180°C (350°F).

Heat oil in a pan. Sear lamb on both sides until caramelised. Arrange garlic, lemongrass and kaffir lime leaves on a baking tray. Place lamb on top. Roast lamb for 4–5 minutes or until lamb is medium-rare. Brush with satay glaze.

Sprinkle a little crushed black pepper on lamb and torch until nicely caramelised.

Prepare peanut sauce. Toast peanuts and cashews in a dry pan. Set aside. Heat garlic, shallots, *kaferia* galangal, kaffir lime leaves, red chillies and bird's eye chillies in a saucepan over medium heat. Add toasted peanuts and cashews and mix well. Remove from heat. Transfer to a food processor. Add some water to aid the movement of the blades and process until a smooth paste is obtained. Season with salt, sugar and brown sugar.

Place peanut sauce on a serving plate and top with chopped peanuts and fried shallots. Place lamb on peanut sauce. Garnish as desired.

BONGSU KIM

Chef, KOREAN BISTRO
21ST CENTURY SEOUL

Seoul, Korea

Contemporary Korean
Bistro cuisine

Cooking style
Bong's style of cooking contemporary Korean bistro cuisine.

Background story behind this dish
This is a typical Korean pork dish that is usually served with *makgeolli* (rice wine). I wanted to give it a contemporary twist.

Biggest achievement
I was lucky enough to work at a Michelin 2-starred restaurant called Jungsik NYC, where my career first took off.

Motivation to becoming a chef
My mum was a chef, so I spent a lot of time in the kitchen when I was young. I fell in love with cooking since then.

Dreams and aspirations
I would like to share typical Korean cooking techniques and ingredients with the world.

Cooking philosophy
Farm to table cooking. Freshness is everything.

Pig's Head Pyeonyuk

Serves 2–4

DONGCHIMI

8 daikon

300 g (11 oz) sea salt

2 litres (64 fl oz / 8 cups) filtered water

4 cloves garlic, peeled and sliced

10 g ($^1/_3$ oz) ginger, peeled

3 green chillies

3 red chillies

1 Korean pear, peeled and sliced

3 Korean spring onions

1 brown onion, peeled and sliced

PYEONYUK

1 pig's head

100 g ($3^1/_2$ oz) *doenjang* (fermented soybean paste)

8 litres (256 fl oz / 32 cups) water

2 bay leaves

5 star anise

1 g ground black pepper

50 g ($1^3/_4$ oz) leek

10 g ($^1/_3$ oz) garlic

10 g ($^1/_3$ oz) salted fermented shrimps

$^1/_2$ tsp perilla oil

$^1/_2$ tsp pumpkin seed oil

4 sorrels

1 tsp roasted pumpkin seeds

1 kg (2 lb 3 oz) dried Korean chive powder

MUSTARD DRESSING

50 g ($1^3/_4$ oz) Dijon mustard

50 g ($1^3/_4$ oz) whole grain mustard

100 ml ($3^1/_2$ fl oz / $^2/_5$ cup) olive oil

100 ml ($3^1/_2$ fl oz / $^2/_5$ cup) rice vinegar

70 g ($2^1/_2$ oz) sugar

70 g ($2^1/_2$ oz) Korean mustard sauce

2 tsp lemon juice

NOTE

Pyeonyuk refers to thinly sliced meat which has been boiled and pressed in Korean cuisine.

Dongchimi is a variety of kimchi often enjoyed in Korean cuisine.

METHOD

Prepare *dongchimi* 1 month ahead. Cut daikon into the shape of a baton and salt with 100 g (3¹/₂ oz) sea salt. Set aside for 3 hours before rinsing. Mix remaining salt with water in a container with a tight-fitting lid.

Place garlic, ginger, green and red chillies, pear, spring onions and onion in a filtering bag. Place bag into salted water and close tightly with lid. Refrigerate to ferment for at least 1 month.

Prepare *pyeonyuk* 1 day ahead. Remove meat from pig head. Mix *doenjang* with water in a pot. Bring meat, bay leaf, star anise, pepper, leek, garlic and shrimps to a boil in *doenjang* mixture. Cook for about 2 hours until meat is tender. Strain meat and set aside. Continue to simmer liquid in pot until reduced by half. Place meat in a mould with reduced jus. Cover with cling wrap. Press with heavy container overnight until liquid sets.

Prepare mustard dressing. Combine all ingredients in a bowl.

Portion *pyeonyuk* and coat with perilla oil and pumpkin seed oil. Crust with sorrel, roasted pumpkin seeds and Korean chive powder. Serve with mustard dressing and *dongchimi*.

DAN HONG

Executive Chef,
MR WONG AND MS G'S

Sydney, Australia

Modern Asian cuisine

Cooking style
Fun and delicious.

Background story behind this dish
I am Vietnamese and I wanted to do a steak tartare dish that had Vietnamese flavours. Lemongrass and fresh herbs like Vietnamese mint and sawtooth coriander give it that fresh touch along with fish sauce and chilli. Egg yolk represents the French influence. It's a very easy dish to prepare at home and makes an excellent starter. You can also serve it with crackers which makes a delicious canapé.

Biggest achievement
Winning the Josephine Pignolet award for Best Young Chef in 2007, as many great chefs have won this award.

Main inspiration
My inspiration comes from everything I eat, whether it is at a local food court, a Michelin-starred restaurant, a restaurant staff meal, a street stall in South East Asia or at my mum's place.

Motivation to becoming a chef
I wasn't good at anything else; I hated studying and flunked high school. I started cooking at home as a kid because my mother owned a Vietnamese restaurant and I always watched her cook. It was my mum who suggested I become a chef and I thought I'd give it a go.

Vietnamese Steak Tartare

Serves 4

400 g (14¹/₃ oz) good quality sashimi-grade beef tri-tip

4 egg yolks

4 Tbsp deep-fried shallots

16 prawn crackers

HERBS

30 coriander leaves, finely sliced

4 sawtooth coriander leaves, finely sliced

30 Vietnamese mint leaves, finely sliced

30 round-leaf mint, finely sliced

20 Thai basil leaves, finely sliced

2 stalks lemongrass, white section only, finely sliced

A bunch of chives, finely chopped

DRESSING

175 ml fish sauce

40 g (1¹/₃ oz) sugar

40 ml lime juice

3¹/₂ Tbsp white vinegar

3 tsp chilli oil

100 ml (3¹/₂ fl oz / ²/₅ cup) grapeseed oil

1 Tbsp *ot tuong* (minced pickled chilli)

TIP
Use the best beef you can get. I use tri-tip in the recipe, but strip loin, fillet, rib-eye and even topside are great substitutes.

METHOD

Prepare dressing. Combine all ingredients in a bowl. Set aside.

Prepare beef. Remove all visible sinew, then cut beef into very small 0.4-cm (¹/₄-in) pieces with a sharp knife.

Combine beef, herbs and 120 ml (4 fl oz / ¹/₂ cup) dressing in a bowl. Mix until well combined. Divide mixture among four plates and shape into a circular mound, making a small dent in the middle.

Place one egg yolk in the dent of each tartare and top with deep-fried shallots.

Serve with prawn crackers.

DAUNGPORN SONGVISAVA

Co-owner and Chef,
BO.LAN
ESSENTIALLY THAI

Bangkok, Thailand

Thai cuisine

Cooking style
Real and fresh.

Background story behind this dish
Green curry is one of the most common curries in Thailand and abroad. However, it is quite difficult to find restaurants that serve authentic and delicious green curry. I chose this recipe to encourage others to make their own paste and cook it at home. There is a marked difference.

Best thing about being a chef
The best thing about being a chef is that we can influence how and what people eat.

Kitchen utensil you can't live without
Mortar and pestle.

Go-to food after a busy dinner service
Soft-boiled egg with fish sauce, sliced chillies and freshly steamed rice.

Green Curry with Chicken

Serves 2–4

240 ml (8 fl oz / 1 cup) fresh coconut cream

200 g (7 oz) chicken feet

2 Tbsp fish sauce

120 ml (4 fl oz / $^1/_2$ cup) chicken stock

65 g ($2^3/_{10}$ oz) pea and apple aubergines, cut into quarters

1 Tbsp palm sugar

A small handful of Thai basil

PASTE

2 coriander roots

1 tsp kaffir lime zest

1 tsp coriander seeds

$^1/_2$ tsp toasted cumin seeds

$^1/_2$ tsp ground white pepper

4 green chillies

2 green bird's eye chillies

$^1/_4$ Tbsp chopped shallots

3 Tbsp roughly chopped garlic

5 Tbsp finely chopped lemongrass

2 Tbsp finely chopped galangal

$^1/_2$ Tbsp shrimp paste

METHOD

Prepare paste. Using a mortar and pestle, pound all ingredients into a paste.

Simmer coconut cream in a pan over medium heat until oil separates. Add paste and stir-fry for 10 minutes until fragrant. Add chicken feet and cook until fragrant. Season with fish sauce. Add chicken stock. Mix well.

Add aubergines. Season with palm sugar. Stir in Thai basil.

Remove from heat. Garnish as desired. Serve.

HAJIME YONEDA

Owner and Chef, HAJIME

Osaka, Japan

Artistic cuisine

Cooking style
Innovative and artistic.

Background story behind this dish
The dish is named *sora*. *Sora* means sky in Japanese. When you look up at the sky, you feel hope. That is why I made this dish with my heart. I also used black garlic purée to trace out birds in flight on the plate as they complement the concept of the dish well.

Earliest memory with food
Playing in the mountains of Japan and eating Japanese knotweed, an edible wild plant. I sometimes prepare this ingredient in a sorbet in my restaurant.

Favourite memory as a chef
This is the story of one guest who would usually visit my restaurant about four times a year with his wife. One day, the guest asked if I knew why they visited my restaurant. He shared that their company was in danger of bankruptcy when they first visited my restaurant and thought it would be their last time doing so. They were served a dish that represented a bud blooming in adversity and it made them cheer up. It has been five years since and their company has emerged from bankruptcy. I always think that "cooking gives hope" and in that moment, my belief was materialised.

Sora

Serves 2–4

1 duck breast

Oil as needed

Salt as needed

2 leeks, thinly sliced into 8-cm (3²/₅-in) lengths and thoroughly cleaned

8 g (¹/₃ oz) butter

A piece of dried orange peel

Ground black pepper as needed

1 clove black garlic, peeled and puréed

2 g spring onion sprouts

METHOD

Preheat oven to 180°C (350°F).

Place duck skin-side down on a clean surface. Using a knife, make a tiny cut through the duck. Be careful not to cut the meat through.

Heat oil in a frying pan over medium heat. Place duck skin-side down in pan and grill until light brown. Remove from heat. Place duck in oven at 180°C (350°F) for 2 minutes. Remove from oven and place duck in oven at 60°C (140°F) for 30 minutes. The duck will continue to cook in the residual heat. Sprinkle salt over duck.

Boil leeks in lightly salted water. Place leeks in butter and season with salt.

Place dried orange peel in a food processor and process until fine.

Heat oil in a frying pan over high heat and grill duck skin-side down. Cut and divide duck into equal portions. Season with black pepper and salt.

Decorate serving plate with silhouettes of birds in flight with black garlic purée if desired. Place duck and leek on plate. Sprinkle ground orange peel over. Garnish with spring onion sprouts and serve.

JIMMY LIM TYAN YAW

Founder and Chef,
JL STUDIO

Taichung, Taiwan

Modern Singaporean
cuisine

Cooking style
Fun and flavourful.

Background story behind this dish
Bak kut teh is a popular pork rib broth dish in Singapore. The name literally translates to *"bak kut"* which is pork rib and *"teh"* which is tea.

Main inspiration
My grandmother. I think I got my instinct for cooking from my grandmother. She had a natural feel for ingredients and everything she cooked always turned out well.

Favourite food city
Singapore, as it is a melting pot of ethnic groups, religions and cultures. Eating is one of the country's national pastimes. I am spoilt for choice. I can have Chinese food for breakfast, Malay food for lunch, Peranakan cakes for tea and Indian food for dinner. Every meal is packed full of amazing flavours.

Most underrated Asian ingredient
I would cast my vote for the curry leaf which is also known as sweet neem leaf. I love how they impart a deliciously nutty aroma to any dish.

Bak Kut Teh

Serves 2–4

BAK KUT TEH

1¹/₂ kg (3 lb 4¹/₂ oz) pork ribs

3 litres (96 fl oz / 12 cups) water

350 g (12²/₅ oz) garlic,
lightly crushed

1 onion

55 g (2 oz) white peppercorns,
crushed

2 pieces *dang gui* (angelica
sinensis), sliced

2 sticks *dang shen* codonopsis
pilosula)

3 slices *chuan xiong* (ligusticum
striatum)

1 star anise

1¹/₂ Tbsp salt

DOUGH FRITTERS

250 g (9 oz) all-purpose flour

1 egg

1 tsp baking powder

3 tsp milk

25 g (⁴/₅ oz) butter, softened

80 ml (2⁴/₅ fl oz / ⁴/₅ cup) water

Oil as needed

DARK SOY SAUCE DIP

Dark soy sauce as needed

Sliced red chillies as needed

TIP
The three main components in this dish are white pepper, garlic and the spices. You may change or adjust the other ingredients to your liking.

METHOD

Prepare dough for the fritters 1 day ahead. Place all ingredients except water and oil in a mixer and mix at low speed. Gradually add water when mixing. Dough should be soft to the touch and not stick to the bowl. Knead dough for 15 minutes. Cover dough with cling wrap and leave to rest overnight in the refrigerator. Bring dough to room temperature before using.

Prepare *bak ku teh*. Blanch pork ribs in a pot of boiling water. Place pork ribs in a pressure cooker with rest of ingredients and bring to a boil. Lower heat and simmer for 50 minutes. If not using a pressure cooker, bring all ingredients in a pot to a boil and simmer for $1^{1}/_{2}$ hours. Strain broth and reserve pork ribs and garlic.

Prepare dough fritters. Heat sufficient oil for deep-frying in a wok until 180°C (350°F). Roll dough out into a thin sheet and cut into 1-cm ($^{1}/_{2}$-in) wide strips. Stack dough strips on top of one another and press centre of dough strips with a chopstick. Hold the ends of each dough strip and gently stretch dough to 25 cm (10 in). Gently lower into oil. Turn dough around in oil and fry until golden brown. Remove from oil and drain on paper towels to remove excess oil.

Place pork ribs, garlic and broth in a warm bowl. Serve with steamed rice, dark soy sauce dip and dough fritters.

JOWETT YU

Chef, HO LEE FOOK

Hong Kong

Eclectic Chinese cuisine

Cooking style
Eclectic Chinese.

Background story behind this dish
It's one of the things my mum taught me how to make. I have vivid memories of making the dumplings together on the weekends when I helped her in the kitchen. After I left home at 18, I'd ask her to make them whenever I came home. When Ho Lee Fook opened, I put it on the menu as homage to her as it was the dish that began my cooking career.

Earliest memory with food
Standing over the wood-fired wok burner in the countryside of Taiwan in my grandmother's kitchen. I remember her showing me an egg and telling me when it was going to hatch by holding it against the sunlight. Sometimes she'd take her shoes off and jump into a tub full of veggies for pickling and walk on them. It was a lot of fun watching her. She was full of knowledge.

Favourite memory as a chef
I think I almost cried when my mum told me my dumplings were better than hers. It was very nice of her to say that and whether it was true or not, it was the best compliment I ever got.

Mum's 'Mostly Cabbage, A Little Bit of Pork' Dumplings

Makes about 100 dumplings

DUMPLINGS

1 cabbage, core removed

1 tsp salt

600 g (1 lb 5¹/₃ oz) pork neck, diced

20 g (²/₃ oz) coriander leaves, roughly chopped

30 g (1 oz) spring onions

20 g (²/₃ oz) grated ginger

5 tsp oyster sauce

1 Tbsp sesame oil

¹/₂ tsp ground white pepper

75 ml (2¹/₂ fl oz / ²/₅ cup) chicken stock

100 white round dumpling skins

DRESSING

Light soy sauce

Zhenjiang vinegar

Chilli flakes

Chilli oil

Sesame oil

Chopped coriander leaves

Chopped spring onions

GARNISH

Coriander leaves

Sliced spring onions

Sliced red chillies

TIP
It is best to prepare and eat the dumplings on the same day as seasoned meat will become drier and tougher the next day.

This recipe makes about 100 dumplings. Any excess dumplings can be kept uncooked in the freezer for up to 3 weeks.

METHOD

Chop cabbage roughly. Rub salt into cabbage with your hands. Squeeze out excess water, then drain and set aside.

Divide diced pork into 2 portions. Using a mixer with a paddle attached, beat 1 portion of diced pork until sticky. This is to give the dumpling a gelatinous texture. Mix beaten pork and cabbage with remaining portion of pork, coriander, spring onions, grated ginger, oyster sauce, sesame oil, pepper and chicken stock to make the dumpling filling.

Prepare dumplings. On a lightly floured tray, place 1 Tbsp pork filling on the centre of a dumpling skin. Dab a little water at the edges and fold skin over to enclose. Using your fingers, create folds and press on edges to seal dumpling. Repeat for remaining dumplings.

To cook dumplings, bring a large pot of water to a boil. Depending on how many dumplings you are cooking at a time, the amount of water and cooking time will vary. Cook dumplings in small batches for about 4 minutes until dumplings float to the surface.

Prepare dressing. As the dressing is a matter of personal taste, the ingredients can be in any proportion according to your preference.

Serve dumplings with dressing. Garnish with coriander, spring onions and sliced red chillies.

KAI HO

Chef de Cuisine, TAÏRROIR

Taipei, Taiwan

Taiwanese-French cuisine

Cooking style
Infinitely creative.

Background story behind this dish
The dish is remarkable as it uses Taiwanese ingredients, but is prepared in a French manner. It is the perfect representation of me on a plate.

Motivation to becoming a chef
I was watching a cooking show on TV when I was in my Junior High years and the show inspired me to become a chef. I love to eat good food as well.

First recipe
Mapo tofu (tofu in spicy Sichuan sauce).

Dreams and aspirations
Introduce more people to beautifully presented Taiwanese food and show them that there's more to our cuisine than just night market or street food.

Earliest memory with food
Peking duck when I was about 5 or 6 years old. The way it was presented really impressed me. The sweet and salty taste of the duck also left a lasting impression on me.

Most underrated Asian ingredient
Rice. It is a staple in Asian food culture.

65°C Egg, Yilan 'Ya Shang' with Taro, Sakura Shrimp and Crispy Shallots

Serves 2–4

1 taro 600–800 g (1 lb 5$^{1}/_{3}$ oz–1$^{3}/_{4}$ lb), peeled and sliced into quarters

6 organic eggs

12 g ($^{1}/_{2}$ oz) dried porcini mushrooms

70 g (2$^{1}/_{2}$ oz) crème fraiche or sour cream

250 ml (8 fl oz / 1 cup) milk

100 g (3$^{1}/_{2}$ oz) unsalted butter

Sea salt as needed

Oil as needed

4 shallots 60 g (2 oz), peeled and chopped

50 g (1$^{3}/_{4}$ oz) fresh or dried sakura shrimps

1 garlic, smashed

50 g (1$^{3}/_{4}$ oz) smoked duck breast, cut into 1-cm ($^{1}/_{2}$-in) cubes

30 g (1 oz) chives, chopped

Ground black pepper to taste

PORCINI OIL

3 g ($^{1}/_{10}$ oz) dried porcini

2 Tbsp grapeseed oil

METHOD

Steam taro for 30 minutes at 100°C (210°F). Cut steamed taro into 1-cm (¹/₂-in) cubes. Pound three quarters into a paste and set remainder aside.

Prepare porcini oil. Mix dried porcini mushrooms with grapeseed oil. Set aside.

Poach eggs at 65°C (150°F) for 50 minutes in a steam oven. Alternatively, boil eggs in salted water for 4–5 minutes, then cover and set aside for 3 minutes.

Preheat oven to 60°C (140°F). Place dried porcini mushrooms in oven for 1 hour until very dry. Transfer porcini to a processor and process until fine.

Place taro paste, crème fraiche or sour cream, milk and butter in a pan over low heat. Stir with a whisk until purée is consistent. Season with salt to taste. Pass purée through a fine sieve. Set aside.

Heat a little oil in a clean pan until 150°C (300°F). Deep-fry shallots until crisp and golden brown. Remove from heat. In the same pan, deep-fry taro cubes until golden brown. Add sakura shrimps and smashed garlic, and sauté until fragrant.

Arrange taro purée, poached eggs, porcini oil and smoked duck breast on a serving plate. Sprinkle porcini powder over. Garnish with deep-fried condiments and chives. Season with salt and ground black pepper.

KENICHI YAMAMOTO

Owner and Chef,
L'ALCHIMISTE

Tokyo, Japan

Traditional French cuisine
with a Modern Approach

Boudin Noir with Parsley Breadcrumbs

Serves 2–4

BOUDIN NOIR

500 g (1 lb 1¹/₂ oz) pork back fat

400 g (14¹/₃ oz) onions, peeled and thinly sliced

20 g (²/₃ oz) garlic, peeled and thinly sliced

150 ml (5 fl oz /³/₅ cup) red wine, more as needed

150 ml (5 fl oz /³/₅ cup) heavy cream

1 litre (32 fl oz / 4 cups) pork blood

20 g (²/₃ oz) salt

6 g ground white pepper

PARSLEY BREADCRUMBS

100 g (3¹/₂ oz) parsley

Boiling water as needed

150 ml (5 fl oz / ³/₅ cup) iced water

Water as needed

100 g (3¹/₂ oz) all-purpose flour

5 g (¹/₆ oz) dried yeast

3 eggs

50 g (1³/₄ oz) unsalted butter

1 tsp salt

Cooking style
French gastronomy.

Biggest achievement
We won the Michelin star in Tokyo.

Dreams and aspirations
I want to bring happiness to more people through my cooking.

Cooking philosophy
Cooking is love.

Kitchen utensil you can't live without
The chef's knife that I've used for 20 years.

Most underrated Asian ingredient
Natto.

Recipe you would make with a jar of soy sauce
Tamagoyaki (Japanese rolled omelette).

METHOD

Prepare *boudin noir*. Place pork back fat in a food processor and process into a paste. Set aside.

Sauté onions and garlic in a medium-sized pot over low heat. Add pork fat paste, red wine and heavy cream. Stir well. Add pork blood. Mix slowly and stir constantly over low heat at approximately 55°C (130°F). Season with salt and pepper.

Preheat oven to 75°C (167°F). Transfer to a food mixer and mix into a fine paste. Strain paste to remove any lumps. Pour into a terrine mould. Bake until internal temperature measures approximately 68°C (154°F).

Prepare parsley breadcrumbs. Place parsley in boiling water for a few seconds. Remove and transfer to iced water. Place parsley and sufficient amount of water in a food processor and process into a purée. Strain purée to remove any lumps.

Place parsley purée in a bowl. Add flour, yeast, eggs, butter and salt. Mix well. Place mixed purée in an *espuma* gun. Let rest in refrigerator for 1 hour or more.

Squeeze parsley foam out into a heatproof cup. Microwave mixture for 45 seconds.

Place cup upside down on a cooling rack until it is just warm. Remove parsley foam from cup and place in a steam convection oven at 85°C (185°F) to dry.

Place mixture in a food processor and process until it resembles breadcrumbs.

Cut *boudin noir* into pieces. Brush with red wine. Sprinkle with parsley breadcrumbs. Bake at 60°C (140°F) for 2 minutes to warm the dish before serving.

NOTE
Boudin noir is a type of blood sausage made with pork and pig's blood.

An *espuma* gun is used to create foam in gourmet kitchens.

TIP
The pig's blood has to be fresh in order for the *boudin noir* to turn out well.

RYUJI TESHIMA

Owner and Chef,
RESTAURANT PAGES

Paris, France

Gastronomic cuisine

Cooking style
French-Japanese fusion.

Background story behind this dish
This dish is very similar to one of the specials in our restaurant. I wanted others to have the opportunity to prepare it from the comfort of their home.

Biggest achievement
The opportunity to work with Hugo Desnoyer.

Cooking philosophy
Always serve something that exceeds our guests' expectations as a professional chef.

Favourite food city
Japan. I love their sushi and grilled eels.

Cooking tips
Practice makes perfect. If you have a dish that you want to master, make it at home as often as you can. Don't worry about perfecting it in the beginning, but just enjoy the learning process.

Slow-cooked Chicken with Poached Egg and White Wine Sauce

Serves 4

Olive oil as needed

2 chicken breasts 400 g (14^1/$_3$ oz), with skin

1 Tbsp butter

200 g (7 oz) quinoa

Bouillon as needed

1 shallot, peeled and minced

4 tsp heavy cream

30 g (1 oz) Parmesan cheese

4 poached eggs

WHITE WINE SAUCE

200 ml (6^3/$_4$ fl oz / ^{4}/$_5$ cup) white wine

90 ml (3 fl oz / ^{3}/$_8$ cup) chicken stock

Salt to taste

Butter to taste

METHOD

Preheat oven to 65°C (150°F).

Heat a grill pan over medium-high heat. Add some olive oil and place chicken skin-side down on pan. Cook until chicken turns golden brown and skin is crisp. Turn chicken over. Add butter and lightly sear other side of chicken.

Place pan in oven and cook for 40 minutes at 65°C (150°F). Remove pan from oven and set chicken aside.

Prepare white wine sauce. Deglaze grill pan with white wine and simmer until sauce is thickened and reduced. Add chicken stock and simmer. Season with salt and butter to taste. Set aside.

Place quinoa and sufficient bouillon to cover quinoa in a pot and bring to a boil for 20 minutes over low heat until quinoa softens. Remove quinoa and mix with minced shallots, heavy cream and Parmesan cheese.

Reheat chicken in a clean grill pan before serving.

Cut chicken into half and serve on a large plate with poached eggs. Place quinoa and herbs or salad of your choice on the side. Drizzle with white wine sauce.

SAM LEONG

Chef, FOREST 森

Singapore

Modern Chinese cuisine

Cooking style
Modern Chinese.

Background story behind this dish
The dish is one of my signature creations that is available at Forest. In Chinese cuisine, soup is traditionally an important component of a meal, and it is also one of the most popular dishes in any Chinese restaurant.

Motivation to becoming a chef
I did not like to study when I was younger. I also did not know what I wanted to do. As my dad was a chef at that time, I decided to train under him. I have never looked back since.

Worst thing about being a chef
Being a chef calls for long hours in the kitchen which is physically demanding and takes a toll on the time spent with my family.

Favourite ingredient
My favourite ingredient to work with is fresh seafood, which has the natural sweetness of the sea which I love and minimises the need for seasoning.

Double-boiled Milky Chicken Broth with Morel Mushroom and Wild Bamboo Pith in Whole Fragrant Coconut

Serves 10

30 morel mushrooms, soaked in cold water for 30 minutes

20 wild bamboo piths, cut into pieces and soaked in cold water for 30 minutes

10 dried scallops, soaked in cold water for 30 minutes

A slice of ginger

1 spring onion

A pinch of salt

30 wolfberries

10 whole young Thai coconuts, flesh removed

MILKY CHICKEN BROTH

500 g (1 lb 1¹/₂ oz) lean pork, cut into pieces

10 chicken feet

1 kg (2 lb 3 oz) chicken (old fowl), cut into pieces

10 litres (320 fl oz / 40 cups) water

SEASONING

¹/₂ tsp salt

¹/₂ tsp sugar

2 Tbsp Shaoxing wine

TIP
If preferred, you may substitute the chicken with duck.

METHOD

Prepare milky chicken broth. Blanch lean pork, chicken feet and chicken together in hot water for about 3 minutes and rinse. Simmer lean pork, chicken feet, chicken and water in a large pot for 3 hours over very low heat. Increase temperature to very high heat and boil for another 30 minutes, stirring continuously. The soup will naturally turn milky in colour. Remove from heat and strain broth. Reserve milky chicken broth for later use.

Drain morel mushrooms and bamboo piths and steam for 20 minutes. Set aside.

Drain dried scallops and add fresh water to the scallops. Add ginger, spring onion and salt, and steam for 45 minutes until tender.

Place morel mushrooms, bamboo piths, scallops and wolfberries in coconut.

Bring 2 litres (64 fl oz / 8 cups) milky chicken broth to a boil. Season with salt to taste. Pour into individual coconuts. Steam for 15 minutes until hot before serving. Garnish as desired.

TONY YOO HYUN SU

Owner and Chef,
DOOREYO

Seoul, Korea

Contemporary Korean
cuisine

Cooking style
Beauty of fermentation.

Background story behind this dish
This dish represents Korea's autumn,
a season where wild mushrooms of
many varieties grow in abundance in the
mountains.

Biggest achievement in your career
The first Seoul edition of the Michelin
Guide was unveiled this year (2016)
and I got the honour of receiving the
Michelin star.

Cooking philosophy
Cooking is just like practising asceticism
in the mountains.

Earliest memory with food
A hot potato steamed by my grandmother.

Favourite ingredient
Fermented vegetables and fermented
soybean sauce.

Jeju Black Pig Ssam with Wild Mushroom and Fermented Soybean Paste

Serves 4–6

5 Tbsp fermented soybean paste

BLACK PIG SSAM

1 pig's head

250 ml (8 fl oz / 1 cup) rice wine

5 shallots, peeled

5 cloves garlic, peeled

Water as needed

2 Tbsp chopped parsley

Salt to taste

Freshly ground pepper to taste

WILD MUSHROOMS AND VEGETABLES

450 g (1 lb) mushrooms
(chanterelles, morels, porcini or
any cultivated mushrooms of your
choice)

450 g (1 lb) wild greens

1 Tbsp olive oil

Salt to taste

Freshly ground pepper to taste

5 Tbsp fine breadcrumbs

1 Tbsp black sesame seeds

1 tsp sesame oil

1 tsp finely chopped garlic

NOTE

Ssam refers to a dish in
Korean cuisine in which leafy
vegetables are used to wrap
a piece of meat such as pork,
beef or chicken.

METHOD

Prepare black pig *ssam* 1 day ahead. Soak pig's head in a large pot of lightly salted water for 10 hours to remove impurities. Drain and rinse head thoroughly.

Preheat oven to 110°C (230°F).

Place head in a large ovenproof pot. Add rice wine, shallots, garlic and enough water to cover ingredients. Cover with a lid and braise in oven for 8 hours. Remove head from liquid and set aside until cool enough to handle. Skim braising liquid and simmer in a pan until reduced by half.

Carefully remove meat and ears from head. Slice ears thinly. Combine meat, ears and parsley in a bowl. Season with salt and pepper. Add reduced braising liquid and pour into a terrine or loaf tin lined with cling wrap. Let set for 1 day.

Prepare wild mushrooms and vegetables. Trim mushrooms and wild greens, wash in cold water and drain well. If mushrooms are large, slice or cut into halves or quarters. Heat olive oil in a large heavy pan over high heat. When oil is very hot and almost smoking, add mushrooms and wild greens and cook until mushrooms are browned and crisp. Season with salt and pepper.

Sprinkle breadcrumbs, black sesame seeds, sesame oil and chopped garlic into pan and toss well for 10 seconds.

To serve, brush fermented soybean paste on a serving plate. Place meat and sliced ears on plate and top with wild mushrooms and wild greens.

XAVIER HSU

Head Chef,
NKU FIREWOOD

Taipei, Taiwan

Firewood cuisine

Cooking style
Balanced and solid.

Background story behind this dish
This dish reminds me of the first time I came into contact with the Ruiyan tribes at Nantou. As a result, I've opted to use local ingredients from Taiwan to pay homage to the tribes.

Motivation to becoming a chef
I was a picky eater when I was a child so I developed discerning taste buds as I grew up. I decided to be a chef after graduating from high school.

Cooking philosophy
By paying attention to each step, I find that my dishes turn out well.

Favourite food city
I love Tokyo. I appreciate that the Japanese are careful and driven and they take pride in everything they do. That is why Japanese food has its own unique flavour.

Favourite ingredient
Lobster.

Pork Belly

Serves 2–4

500 g (1 lb 1½ oz) pork belly, washed

Oil as needed

200 g (7 oz) onions, peeled and cut into chunks

100 g (3½ oz) celery, cut into chunks

100 g (3½ oz) carrots, peeled and cut into chunks

100 g (3½ oz) chorizo, cut into chunks

150 ml (5 fl oz / ³⁄₅ cup) red wine

100 g (3½ oz) tomato sauce

10 g (⅓ oz) tomato paste

50 g (1¾ oz) pigeon peas, soaked overnight

500 ml (16 fl oz / 2 cups) chicken stock

Salt to taste

Sugar to taste

SPICE BRINE

1 litre (32 fl oz / 4 cups) water

40 g (1⅓ oz) sea salt

40 g (1⅓ oz) sugar

20 g (⅔ oz) garlic, peeled

5 g (⅙ oz) thyme

2 bay leaves

10 white peppercorns

6 *magau* (Taiwanese black peppercorns)

TIP
Prepare all the ingredients and stew them for 1½ hours. *Magau* is a lemon-scented black peppercorn native to Taiwan. Black peppercorns can be used as a substitute.

METHOD

Prepare pork belly 1 day ahead. Soak pork belly in spice brine overnight.

Heat oil in a pot over medium heat. Fry onions, celery, carrots and chorizo until golden and tender. Add red wine, tomato sauce, tomato paste, pigeon peas and chicken stock. Bring to a boil. Season with salt and sugar to taste.

Sear pork belly for 1 minute on each side in a dry pan. Add pork belly to stock and simmer over low heat for 1^1/$_2$ hours.

Remove pork belly and allow to cool before handling. Cut into thick slices and grill for 1 minute on each side.

Garnish as desired. Serve.

YOON HWAYOUNG

Co-owner and Chef,
RESTAURANT MERCIEL

Busan, Korea

French-Korean cuisine

Cooking style
Classic French, using seasonal ingredients from Korea.

Background story behind this dish
This is a very classical way of preparing lamb, but I added my own twist by using Korean chives instead of the conventional mint or basil.

Cooking philosophy
My philosophy is to create recipes which represent myself as a chef so that my diners can enjoy dishes which represent me.

Kitchen utensil you can't live without
Salt shaker.

Favourite memory as a chef
I prepared my son's first meal when he was a baby.

Cooking tip
Master your basics faithfully.

Lamb with Korean Chives

Serves 4

8 lamb chops from French rack

KOREAN CHIVE PISTOU

200 g (7 oz) Korean chives

100 ml (3½ fl oz / ⅖ cup) extra virgin olive oil

2 cloves garlic

Zest from 1 lemon

5 g (⅙ oz) *piment d'Espelette* (red chilli pepper powder)

SHERRY VINAIGRETTE

90 ml (3 fl oz / ⅜ cup) extra virgin olive oil

2 Tbsp sherry vinegar

Lamb jus (optional)

Salt to taste

Ground black pepper to taste

1 tomato, peeled and cut into small cubes

WHITE BEAN RAGOUT

200 g (7 oz) *paimpol* haricot beans

400 ml (13½ fl oz / 1⅗ cups) water

400 ml (13½ fl oz / 1⅗ cups) chicken stock

Butter as needed

Chopped parsley as needed

METHOD

Prepare Korean chive pistou. Combine all ingredients in a food processor and process into a purée. Mix well and set aside.

Prepare sherry vinaigrette. Mix olive oil and sherry vinegar together in a bowl. Add remaining ingredients except tomato. Mix well and toss with tomato cubes. Set aside.

Prepare white bean ragout. Cook beans with water and chicken stock in a pot over medium heat. Bring to a boil. Reduce heat and simmer bean ragout for about 30–45 minutes until tender. Heat butter in a pan over medium heat. Cook white bean ragout for a few minutes. Add chopped parsley.

Pan-fry or grill lamb over charcoal for 3 minutes on each side until medium rare.

Place lamb on a serving plate. Serve with Korean chive pistou, sherry vinaigrette and white bean ragout.

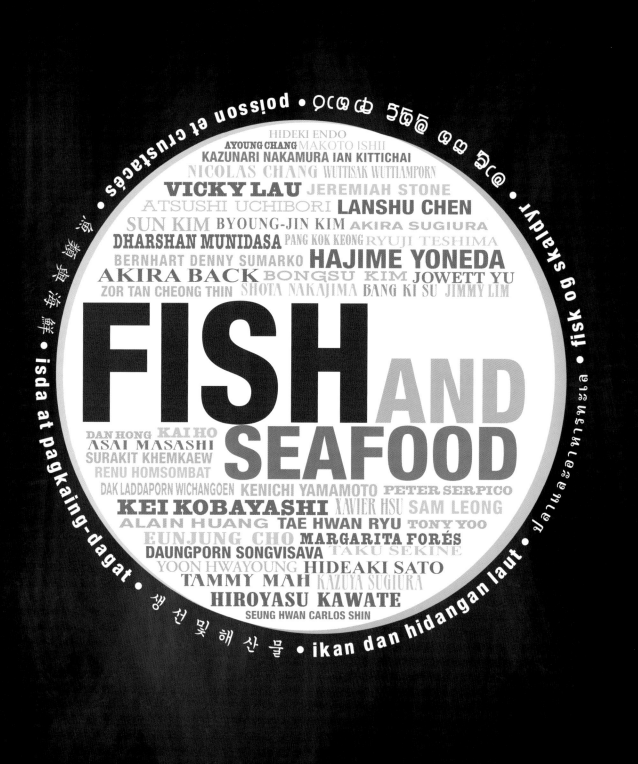

Akira Back
POPCORN AMADAI | 50

Akira Sugiura
MACKEREL FISH FILLET WITH VINEGAR, SHISO LEAVES AND DASHI BROTH JELLY | 52

Byoung-jin Kim
STEAMED ABALONE | 54

Dak Laddaporn Wichangoen
FROZEN RED CURRY WITH LOBSTER | 56

Dharshan Munidasa
PEPPER CRAB | 58

Hideaki Sato
KEGANI CRAB AND AVOCADO COCKTAIL WITH
BLACK VINEGAR SAUCE AND CHRYSANTHEMUM JELLY | 60

Hideki Endo
UNI SEAWEED TACOS WITH FRESH TRUFFLE SEAWEED TACOS | 62

Jeremiah Stone
SQUID MI-CUIT WITH PEPPERS AND NDUJA VINAIGRETTE | 64

Kazuya Sugiura
JOHN DORY WITH GREEN PEA SAUCE AND LEMON CONFIT | 66

Lanshu Chen
AYU, YAMAZERI AND SILVER HERRING | 68

Margarita Forés
CRAB MILHOJAS OF WATER SPINACH GNOCCO AND CALAMONDIN GEL | 70

Renu Homsombat
YUM PLA SALMON | 72

Seung Hwan Carlos Shin
OCTOPUS IN JEREZ VINEGAR WITH SWEET POTATO AND SMOKED PAPRIKA | 74

Surakit Khemkaew
DRIED TROUT WITH WATERMELON | 76

Taku Sekine
SCALLOPS WITH APPLE AND KOMBAWA | 78

Wuttisak Wuttiamporn
MARINATED SALMON WITH KAFFIR LIME LEAVES | 80

Vicky Lau
BOTAN EBI IN SHRIMP AND LEMONGRASS CONSOMMÉ WITH
OSTERA SCHRENCKI CAVIAR AND BAFUN UNI | 83

AKIRA BACK

Owner and Executive Chef,
YELLOWTAIL JAPANESE
RESTAURANT

Las Vegas, USA

Japanese cuisine

Cooking style
Innovative and fresh.

Biggest achievement
My biggest achievement in my professional career was opening up my namesake Akira Back Restaurants in New Delhi and Jakarta, with more opening in Toronto, Singapore, Dubai and Bangkok.

Main inspiration
My mother. I hope to be able to cook as well as she does.

Cooking philosophy
My philosophy in the kitchen is to hire chefs that are more talented than I am. They bring fresh ideas to me and we create as a team.

Dreams and aspirations
I just want to be happy.

Earliest memory with food
My mother always tried to feed me seafood when I was younger and I had not built a taste for it yet. She used to hide candy flavours in the fish so I would eat it.

Worst thing about being a chef
The hardest part about being a chef and having global operations is being away from my family.

Go-to food after a busy dinner service
I like to eat American-style turkey sandwiches.

Popcorn Amadai

Serves 10

1 *amadai* (tilefish) 50–60 g (2 oz), cleaned

Grapeseed oil as needed

SALT WATER BATH

900 ml (30 fl oz / 3⁴/₅ cups) water

35 g (1¹/₅ oz) salt

2–4 small pieces kombu

LEMONGRASS AIR

330 g (11³/₅ oz) lemongrass, chopped

1 white onion, peeled and cut into large chunks

170 g (5²/₃ oz) unsalted butter

670 ml (22³/₅ fl oz / 2⁴/₅ cups) Akira Back sake or regular sake

2 kaffir lime leaves

835 ml (28¹/₅ fl oz / 3¹/₂ cups) heavy whipping cream

5 lemons, halved

Sea salt to taste

Ground white pepper to taste

Lecithin powder or foam stabiliser as needed

Lemon juice to taste

BASIL GEL

100 ml (3¹/₂ fl oz / ²/₅ cup) chicken stock

15 g (¹/₂ oz) unsalted butter, cut into cubes

1 g agar agar powder

185 g (6¹/₂ oz) basil leaves, blanched and processed with just enough water into a smooth purée

Sea salt to taste

Ground white pepper to taste

METHOD

Prepare lemongrass air. Sweat lemongrass and onion with butter in a medium stockpot over low heat until onions are transparent and lemongrass is soft. Add sake and kaffir lime leaves and reduce until almost dry. Add whipping cream and lemons, then bring to a boil. Remove from heat. Cover tightly with cling wrap and let steep for 20–25 minutes.

Strain mixture into a pan and bring to a simmer. Add salt, pepper and lecithin powder or foam stabiliser. Season with lemon juice if needed. Keep in a warm place. Use an immersion hand blender to introduce air.

Prepare basil gel. Bring chicken stock and butter to a boil in a small pot and whisk in agar agar. Continue whisking slowly, adding in basil purée while holding the pot over an ice bath. Season with salt and pepper. Allow to cool for at least 2–4 hours. Blend basil gel until smooth. Place in a squeeze bottle until ready to use.

Prepare salt water bath. Place water and salt in a large pot and allow kombu to infuse for 4 hours.

Preheat oven to 160°C (320°F).

Soak *amadai* in salt water bath, scale-side only. Pat dry with a kitchen towel. Using a skewer, pull *amadai* straight so that it does not curl.

Place *amadai* skin-side up in a baking pan. Heat grapeseed oil in a pan to 60°C (140°C) and pour oil over skin.

Bake *amadai* for 4–6 minutes.

Serve *amadai* with lemongrass air and basil gel. Garnish as desired.

AKIRA SUGIURA

Executive Chef, LUMEN

Paris, France

Italian-Japanese Fusion
cuisine

Cooking style
Multicultural and refined.

Motivation to becoming a chef
The idea of becoming a chef came to
my mind the very first time my parents
brought me to an Italian trattoria in Japan.

Cooking philosophy
I encourage my team to express their
creativity and to share with me their
feelings and ideas about the dishes I create
on a daily basis.

First recipe you ever made
When I was a child I wanted to cook dinner
for my parents, but the only ingredient
that I found in the fridge was eggs. Hence,
I tried to make my parents the best
omelette that they ever had.

Favourite food city
Paris. This city is the symbol of
gastronomy. I like that it offers both
traditional and modern cuisine.

Favourite ingredient
Olive oil because of its scent and flavour
and the fact that it can bind a lot of other
ingredients together.

Most underrated Asian ingredient
Ichiyaboshi (dried mackerel strips).

Mackerel Fish Fillet with Vinegar, Shiso Leaves and Dashi Broth Jelly

Serves 6

6 mackerel fish fillets

Salt as needed

Sugar as needed

300 g (11 oz) Japanese white rice,
washed thrice then soaked for
30 minutes

300 ml (10 fl oz / 1¼ cups)
cold water

35 ml (1⅕ fl oz) sushi vinegar

Shiso powder as needed

Olive oil as needed

Dried sakura leaves or sawdust

DASHI BROTH JELLY

2 tsp dashi powder

2 litres (64 fl oz / 8 cups) water

25 g (⅘ oz) gelatin sheet

NOTE
Shiso is a plant of the mint
family that is used as a herb
in Japanese cooking.

METHOD

Place fillets in a tray and season with salt and sugar. Set aside to marinate for 12 minutes.

Rinse fillets and place on a grill above a gastronome tray. Turn on grill and cover with a lid. Turn off heat and once smoke develops, remove lid and smoke fish for 15 minutes.

Use a torch to grill skin for 15 seconds. Place fillets in refrigerator to stop cooking process.

Bring rice and cold water to a boil over high heat in a large heavy-bottomed pan. Reduce heat to low, cover with a lid and allow rice to cook for 11 minutes. Add sushi vinegar and mix well. Place rice in refrigerator or in front of a fan to dry. Add some shiso powder.

Prepare dashi broth jelly. Mix dashi powder and water in a pot. Bring dashi to a boil over high heat. Stir often. Add gelatin and remove from heat. Stir until gelatin is melted. Remove from heat. Place dashi broth jelly in refrigerator.

Spread rice out on a serving plate. Slice fish very thinly and place on rice. Top with dashi broth jelly, a bit of olive oil and dried sakura leaves or sawdust.

BYOUNG-JIN KIM

Executive Chef, GAON

Seoul, Korea

Korean cuisine

Cooking style
Focus and simplicity.

Background story behind this dish
As abalone has a natural flavour of its own, I focused on presenting the ingredient in the simplest way possible without using any other ingredients to overpower its natural flavours.

Biggest achievement
To receive 3 Michelin stars. It has been a long journey of tears and joy.

Dreams and aspirations
To have a deeper understanding of Korean cuisine through history and to educate many chefs about Korean cuisine.

Earliest memory with food
My mother's fermented soybean stew. She used Korean dried sardine stock and seasoned it with fermented shrimp sauce and pepper. Till now, it remains my favourite food.

Favourite dish
Sogogi mu kuk (beef radish soup).

Dish you would make with a jar of soy sauce
Ganjang gyejang (crab fermented in soy sauce).

Steamed Abalone

Serves 2

2 whole abalones about 110 g (4 oz) each, thoroughly cleaned

2 shiitake mushrooms

SOY SAUCE SEASONING
2 cloves garlic, peeled

20 g (²/₃ oz) leek

50 g (1³/₄ oz) onions

100 ml (3¹/₂ fl oz / ²/₅ cup) soy sauce

4 Tbsp mirin

4 Tbsp malt extract

600 ml (20¹/₄ fl oz / 2¹/₂ cups) water

¹/₄ Korean pear, peeled

ABALONE INTESTINE SAUCE
8 g (¹/₃ oz) cooked abalone intestines

100 ml (3¹/₂ fl oz / ²/₅ cup) clam stock

5 g (¹/₆ oz) ground glutinous rice

5 g (¹/₆ oz) seaweed, finely chopped

Light soy sauce to taste

METHOD

Prepare soy sauce seasoning. Place garlic, leek and onions directly on fire until charred. Combine remaining ingredients and charred ingredients in a pot. Bring to a boil. Remove from heat. Set aside to cool.

Bring abalones, 500 ml (16 fl oz / 2 cups) soy sauce seasoning and shiitake mushrooms to a boil in a pressure cooker. Turn down heat for 1 minute. Turn stove off and set pot aside until all the air is released from the pressure cooker.

Separate abalone meat from intestines.

Prepare abalone intestine sauce. Blend cooked abalone intestines with clam stock and ground glutinous rice, then pass it through a fine sieve. Add chopped seaweed. Bring mixture in a pot to a boil until sauce is heated through. Finish with a drizzle of soy sauce.

Score whole abalone, then cut into 4 pieces.

Serve abalone with abalone intestine sauce.

DAK LADDAPORN WICHANGOEN

Head Chef, KIIN KIIN

Copenhagen, Denmark

Modern Thai cuisine

Cooking style
Innovative Thai.

Background story behind this dish
This dish best represents Kiin Kiin and the type of restaurant we are. With this dish, we have taken something that is synonymous with Thai cuisine and turned it into something new by playing with the textures and the presentation.

Best thing being a chef
I think it is so amazing that you can bring a person back to a memory through something so basic as food. That is what drives me.

Biggest achievement
To work with the food that I have grown up with, and mix it with all the techniques that I have learned working in Kiin Kiin.

Biggest misconception about Asian cuisine
That it needs either to be overflowing with soy sauce, extremely spicy or covered in sweet and sour tomato or pineapple sauce. Especially in Denmark, people tend to go to Chinese or Asian restaurants thinking that the Asian food that they are having is what we Asians eat. A lot of people think that Asian food is all about spring rolls, noodles or anything deep-fried. Asian cuisine is balanced. You need to always have the five tastes in mind when you cook– sweet, sour, bitter, salty and umami.

Frozen Red Curry with Lobster

Serves 2

1 lobster or langoustine, claws and tail only

Chopped cashews

4 fresh longans or lychees, seeded and divided into quarters

RED CURRY PASTE

60 g (2 oz) shrimp paste

5 small red shallots, peeled

10 cloves garlic, peeled

100 g (3¹/₂ oz) red chillies, seeded

150 g (5¹/₃ oz) lemongrass

10 black peppercorns

20 coriander roots

30 lime leaves

1 galangal

2 Tbsp coriander seeds

2 Tbsp dried shrimps

Zest and juice from 2 limes

18 g (³/₅ oz) Thai basil

CURRY SAUCE

2 Tbsp oil

3 litres (96 fl oz / 12 cups) coconut milk

700 g (1¹/₂ lb) condensed milk

Fish sauce to taste

Juice from 3 limes

AVOCADO PURÉE

2 avocados, peeled and seeded

12 g (¹/₂ oz) Thai basil

Salt to taste

Sugar to taste

Juice from 1 lime

TIP
Using an ice cream maker would result in a sauce that has a smoother consistency.

METHOD

Prepare red curry paste. Combine all ingredients in a food processor and process into a smooth paste.

Prepare curry sauce. Heat oil in a wok over medium heat. Stir-fry red curry paste until fragrant. Add coconut milk, condensed milk, fish sauce and lime juice, a little at a time. Remove from heat and let cool. Freeze sauce in an ice cream maker and store frozen. Alternatively, place sauce in the freezer.

Prepare avocado purée. Combine avocados and Thai basil in a food processor and process until smooth and creamy. Season with salt, sugar and lime juice.

Boil lobster or langoustine tail for 2 minutes. Boil claws for 3 minutes.

Place boiled lobster or langoustine pieces on a serving plate. Arrange cashews with longan as desired. Serve with a scoop of frozen red curry and avocado purée. Garnish as desired.

DHARSHAN MUNIDASA

Owner and Chef,
MINISTRY OF CRAB

Colombo, Sri Lanka

Seafood

Cooking style
Ingredient-obsessed.

Background story behind this dish
This dish is a good way of preparing crabs without using the more conventional methods of steaming, boiling and serving in butter.

Biggest achievement
Being recognised by the Japanese government for spreading Japanese culture outside of Japan.

Best thing about being a chef
I am lucky to now have three distinct kitchens namely Japanese, Sri Lankan and Seafood. Each of these kitchens procure the best ingredients available, so much so that two restaurants have a no-freezer policy.

Worst thing about being a chef
I never get invited to people's houses for dinner anymore!

Favourite food city
Tokyo because it is the nexus of all great ingredients. For example, Japan produces the world's best beef, tuna, urchin, salmon roe, pork, fruits and vegetables.

Favourite ingredient
Tuna. Regal big-eyed tuna, as it has so many parts to work with. From its skin to its bones, eyes, belly and jaw, all these parts have various tastes and textures. You realise this when you have access to whole tuna.

Pepper Crab

Serves 2–4

PEPPER STOCK
50 g (1³/₄ oz) black peppercorns
1 litre (32 fl oz / 4 cups) water
3¹/₂ Tbsp oyster sauce

CRAB
3 tsp sunflower oil
1 Tbsp chopped garlic
1 Tbsp chopped onions

1 tsp crushed black pepper
500–600 g (1 lb 1¹/₂ oz–1 lb 5¹/₃ oz) crab, cleaned
15 g (¹/₂ oz) cornflour, mixed with some water into a slurry

METHOD

Prepare pepper stock. Bring black peppercorns and water in a pot to a boil. Simmer liquid in pot until reduced by half. Add oyster sauce and mix well.

Prepare crab. Heat sunflower oil in a wok over medium heat. Add garlic, onions, crushed pepper, pepper stock and crab to wok. Sauté for 13–15 minutes. Add cornflour slurry to thicken sauce.

Dish out and serve.

HIDEAKI SATO

Co-Owner and Chef,
TA VIE

Hong Kong

French-Japanese cuisine

Background story behind this dish
This dish represents my cuisine well.
French cuisine combined with the
philosophy of Japanese cuisine (pure,
simple and seasonal) and featuring
Asian ingredients.

Main inspiration
My mentor chef Seiji Yamamoto (Ryugin).
He loves cooking more than anyone else.

Dreams and aspirations
I would like to travel the world and cook
for as many people as I can.

Favourite food city
Tokyo. I cannot imagine any other city
which has more food choices than Tokyo.

Best thing about being a chef
We get to cook and travel at the same time.

Most underrated Asian ingredient
Tea. There is a very strong tea-drinking
culture in the world and I believe that more
can be done to incorporate this ingredient
in our dishes.

Go-to food after a busy dinner service
Noodles like udon, soba and ramen.

Kegani Crab and Avocado Cocktail with Black Vinegar Sauce and Chrysanthemum Jelly

Serves 8

100 g (3^1/$_2$ oz) crab meat

15 g (^{1}/$_2$ oz) crab miso (crab liver
cooked with a bit of sake)

15 g (^{1}/$_2$ oz) cucumber, peeled
and diced

3 g ginger, peeled and diced

8 slices avocado, peeled

Salt to taste

Lemon juice to taste

BLACK VINEGAR MAYONNAISE

1 egg yolk

8 g (^{1}/$_3$ oz) Dijion mustard

2 tsp Chinese black vinegar

1 tsp sherry vinegar

190 ml (6^2/$_5$ fl oz / ^{4}/$_5$ cup) olive oil

1 tsp salt

CHRYSANTHEMUM JELLY

3 g (^{1}/$_{10}$ oz) kombu

150 g (5^1/$_3$ oz) water

1 Tbsp rice vinegar

1 tsp sherry vinegar

1^1/$_2$ tsp salt

5 g (^{1}/$_6$ oz) sugar

8 g (^{1}/$_3$ oz) chrysanthemum
flowers, blanched in boiling water
for 1 minute then drained

5 g (^{1}/$_6$ oz) agar agar powder

TIP
Using ripe avocados
will enhance the creamy
texture of this dish.

METHOD

Prepare black vinegar mayonnaise. Combine all ingredients in a bowl and mix well. Set aside.

Prepare chrysanthemum jelly 1 day ahead. Soak kombu in water overnight. Bring all ingredients to a boil in a pan. Remove from heat, then pour into 10 cm (4 in) round moulds on a cold tray.

Combine crab meat with 3$^1/_2$ Tbsp black vinegar mayonnaise, crab miso, cucumber and ginger in a bowl. Mix well.

Season avocado with salt and lemon juice to taste.

Serve crab meat with avocado and chrysanthemum jelly.

HIDEKI ENDO

Executive Chef,
MATSUHISA PARIS,
LE ROYAL MONCEAU

Paris, France

Japanese cuisine

Cooking style
First impressions are very important so I make it a point to impress diners with my plating.

Background story behind this dish
I was working at NOBU in Hong Kong for 10 years. The local diners loved to eat sea urchin so I wanted to make finger food out of that!

Main inspiration
Nobu Matsuhisa because he has passion, vision and respect for people and food.

Cooking philosophy
Keep calm and concentrate.

Best thing about being a chef
Seeing the happy smiles of my diners.

Earliest memory with food
Salmon egg *donburi* (rice bowl) from my hometown.

Favourite ingredient
Wagyu beef.

Kitchen utensil you can't live without
My knives. They are specially handmade for me as I am left-handed.

Go-to food after a busy dinner service
Salmon *ochazuke* (rice in green tea).

Uni Seaweed Tacos with Fresh Truffle Seaweed Tacos

Serves 4

Melted Parmesan cheese as needed

$^{1}/_{2}$ lime

SEAWEED TACOS
200 ml ($6^{3}/_{4}$ fl oz / $^{4}/_{5}$ cup) iced water

100 g ($3^{1}/_{2}$ oz) tempura flour

30 g (1 oz) squid ink

Vegetable oil as needed

4 pieces seaweed (*nori*), halved

TRUFFLE TERIYAKI SAUCE
300 ml (10 fl oz / $1^{1}/_{4}$ cups) chicken stock

$3^{1}/_{2}$ Tbsp shoyu (Japanese soy sauce)

$3^{1}/_{2}$ Tbsp mirin (rice wine)

50 g ($1^{3}/_{4}$ oz) sugar

1 Tbsp *kuzu*, mixed with 1 Tbsp water into a paste

2 tsp black truffle oil

1 Tbsp chopped fresh truffles

CREAMY UNI SAUCE
1 egg yolk

1 tsp rice vinegar

105 ml grapeseed oil

1 tsp sea salt

Ground white pepper as needed

50 g ($1^{3}/_{4}$ oz) *uni* (sea urchin) soy sauce

12 g ($^{1}/_{2}$ oz) *uni* (sea urchin) paste

UNI RICE
50 g ($1^{3}/_{4}$ oz) sushi rice

48 g ($1^{4}/_{5}$ oz) snow crab meat

5 g ($^{1}/_{6}$ oz) chopped chives

1 tsp black truffle oil

12 g ($^{1}/_{2}$ oz) fresh *uni* (sea urchin)

GARNISH
Sliced fresh truffles

Coriander sprouts

NOTE
Kuzu is a traditional starch that is widely used in Japan as a thickener.

METHOD

Prepare seaweed tacos. Combine iced water, tempura flour and squid ink in a bowl and mix lightly.

Heat sufficient oil for deep-frying in a wok until 170°C (330°F). Dip seaweed in batter, then fry until crisp. Place immediately into a taco shell basket, then fry again until completely crisp. Repeat with remaining ingredients.

Prepare truffle teriyaki sauce. Place chicken stock, shoyu, mirin and sugar in a pan over medium heat. Stir for 5 minutes or until sugar has dissolved. Add *kuzu* paste and mix. Stir in truffle oil and chopped truffles. Mix well. Remove from heat and allow sauce to cool to room temperature.

Prepare creamy *uni* sauce. Beat egg yolk in a dry bowl. Add rice vinegar followed by oil, a little at a time, then blend thoroughly using a whisk. When mixture starts to thicken, season with salt and pepper. Stir in *uni* soy sauce and *uni* paste. Mix well.

Prepare *uni* rice. Mix all ingredients except *uni* in a bowl. Add 2 Tbsp creamy *uni* sauce. Shape rice into 4 balls. Stuff rice into seaweed tacos. Top with a slice of *uni*.

Drizzle Parmesan cheese and truffle teriyaki sauce over fresh *uni*. Serve with lime. Garnish with fresh truffle slices and coriander sprouts.

JEREMIAH STONE

Co-owner and Chef,
CONTRA and WILDAIR

New York, USA

Modern-American cuisine

Cooking style
Simple and honest.

Background story behind this dish
This dish is made from barely cooked squid so it is still nice and tender. I like this dish because it's simple but yet it also offers a nice play on different textures with the squid and peppers.

Biggest achievement
Opening Contra because I did it with my partner Fabian and we were up against a lot of odds. It was really a passion project that we built from the ground up.

Cooking philosophy
Enjoy cooking, cook with your intuition and never settle for mediocrity when it comes to creating a recipe.

Worst thing about being a chef
The hours and missing family time.

Earliest memory with food
Making dumplings on my mum's lap when I was 4 years old. We used to make dumplings twice a week and I would make the worst looking shapes just because I wanted to experiment.

What you would make with a jar of soy sauce
I would make soy sauce and tea-braised eggs. It's one of my favourite recipes.

Squid Mi-cuit with Peppers and Nduja Vinaigrette

Serves 2–4

455 g (16 oz) squid, thinly sliced

Olive oil as needed

Salt as needed

2 red bell peppers

80 g (2⁴/₅ oz) yuzu *kosho*

A handful of Thai basil

25 g (⁴/₅ oz) toasted sourdough breadcrumbs

NDUJA VINAIGRETTE

50 g (1³/₄ oz) *nduja* (spicy pork spread)

4 Tbsp olive oil

245 g (8³/₅ oz) fermented pineapple (see note), reserve fermented liquid

4 Tbsp white wine vinegar

NOTE

Yuzu *kosho* is a type of Japanese seasoning usually made from chilli, yuzu zest and salt.

If fermented pineapple is not available in stores, prepare your own by fermenting pineapple cubes from 1 pineapple with sugar (2% of pineapple's weight) for 3 days.

TIP

If you are unable to find *nduja*, you may use a Calabrian chilli spread containing anchovies and garlic as a substitute.

METHOD

Preheat oven to 200°C (400°F). Place squid on a baking tray and drizzle with olive oil. Season with salt. Bake for 15 minutes until just tender and a little opaque.

Char bell peppers over a fire. Place in a bowl and cover to allow bell peppers to soften. Remove charred bits and seeds. Slice thinly into 7.5 × 0.5-cm (3 x ¹/₄-in) lengths.

Prepare *nduja* vinaigrette. Place *nduja* in a pot over low heat. Remove from heat and mix with olive oil. Set aside. Blend fermented pineapple with reserved liquid and white wine vinegar. Strain and add to *nduja* to make a warm vinaigrette.

Mix squid and bell peppers together with a small amount of yuzu *kosho* and olive oil. Place onto a serving plate and layer Thai basil in between. Spoon *nduja* vinaigrette over and top with toasted sourdough crumbs.

KAZUYA SUGIURA

Chef, MARKT

Tokyo, Japan

Neo-Natural cuisine

Dreams and aspirations
To be able to cook all over the world.

Cooking philosophy
Be natural.

Best thing about being a chef
Every day is a new and incredibly exciting experience.

Earliest memory with food
Japanese local food.

Biggest misconception about Asian cuisine
That good Asian food can only be found in Asian countries. In fact, good Asian food can be found in Europe and even Africa.

Motivation to becoming a chef
I admire chefs.

Favourite food cities
Paris, New York and Tokyo.

First dish you ever made
Breakfast for my mother.

What you would make with a jar of soy sauce
You can make anything!

John Dory with Green Pea Sauce and Lemon Confit

Serves 2–4

Olive oil as needed

1¹/₂–2 kg (4 lb 6 oz) John Dory fillet, skinned

Butter as needed

8–10 oxalis leaves

SALTY LEMON CONFIT

3 lemons

150 g (5¹/₃ oz) salt

75 g (2³/₅ oz) sugar

Water as needed

SWEET LEMON CONFIT

3 lemons, cut into 1-cm (¹/₂-in) thick slices

80 g (2⁴/₅ oz) sugar

GREEN PEA SAUCE

250 g (9 oz) green peas

A pinch of salt

500 g (1 lb 1¹/₂ oz) clams

Ginger as needed

Shallots as needed, peeled

White wine as needed

METHOD

Prepare salty lemon confit 2 months ahead. Score a cross on lemons but do not slice entirely. Rub salt and sugar into lemons and place in a clean jar. Cover with remaining salt and sugar. Fill jar with water and seal tightly. Refrigerate for 2 months before using. Boil skin of lemons to remove salt. Rinse before slicing.

Prepare sweet lemon confit. Marinate lemons with sugar for 1 hour. Place lemon and sugar in a pan and bring to a boil. Reduce until one-third of original amount. Transfer to a food processor and blend into a purée. Pass confit through a strainer.

Prepare green pea sauce. Boil green peas in a pot of lightly salted water until tender. Drain and plunge immediately into iced water to retain colour of the peas.

Place clams, ginger, shallots and white wine in a pan and simmer over medium heat until clams open up. Extract essence of clams.

Process essence of clams and green peas in a food processor until smooth. Heat butter in a pan and add blended pea mixture. Whisk sauce. Set aside.

Heat olive oil in a medium-sized pan over medium heat. Place John Dory fillet in pan and cook until just done and tender. Remove from heat.

Serve John Dory fillet with salty lemon confit, sweet lemon confit and green pea sauce. Garnish with oxalis leaves.

LANSHU CHEN

Owner and Chef, LE MOUT

Taichung, Taiwan

French Haute cuisine

Cooking style
I like to test and develop flavours from different produce that are in season. Whether the flavours clash or are balanced, the result is a brand new sensation.

Background story behind this dish
This dish perfectly represents my cooking style. I love that the silver herring has a smoky umami taste that is in total contrast with the grassy texture of the *yamazeri* purée. The flavours are unexpected but yet, go so well together.

Main inspiration
Chef Jean-François Piège, who inspired me with his amazing artistic balance of flavours and extremely exquisite presentation. His work in Les Ambassadeurs during the Hotel de Crillon period is the epitome of French haute cuisine.

Favourite ingredient
Fermented bean curd paste as it is savoury, sweet and spicy.

Cooking philosophy
During my time in France, an important concept I learned was to respect food, respect guests and respect yourself. In Taiwan and China, being a chef doesn't sound like a very sexy job. Most of the older generation see it as an inferior choice of career. For me, however, being a professional chef allows me to share my feelings, passion and memories with so many people, directly and sincerely.

Ayu, Yamazeri and Silver Herring

Serves 10

5 *ayu* (sweet fish), opened from belly and deboned

AYU MOUSSE
100 g (3¹/₂ oz) *ayu* (sweet fish) fillet, bones and head reserved

Oil as needed

Salt to taste

20 g (²/₃ oz) egg whites

10 g (¹/₃ oz) pork fat

10 g (¹/₃ oz) ice cubes

SAKE GEL
100 ml (3¹/₂ fl oz / ²/₅ cup) water

2 g agar agar powder

3 Tbsp sake

MISO CREAM
10 g (¹/₃ oz) egg yolk

3 Tbsp grapeseed oil

5 tsp argan oil

Salt to taste

1 tsp lemon juice

35 g (1¹/₅ oz) white miso paste

FISH FUMET
100 g (3¹/₂ oz) *ayu* (sweet fish) bones

10 g (¹/₃ oz) kombu

300 ml (10 fl oz / 1¹/₄ cups) cold water

30 g (1 oz) dried baby silver herrings

SILVER HERRING PASTE
50 g (1³/₄ oz) dried baby silver herrings, soaked in warm water for 10 minutes

Oil as needed

50 g (1³/₄ oz) fish fumet

5 g (¹/₆ oz) squid ink

YAMAZERI PURÉE
Water as needed

Salt as needed

200 g (7 oz) *yamazeri* leaves, blanched for 3 seconds, placed immediately into iced water then drained

GARNISH
Pickled onion petals as needed

Baby oyster leaves as needed

TIP
Ayu fillet weighs between 200 g (7 oz) and 400 g (14¹/₃ oz) a piece, depending on the size of the fish.

If you cannot find *yamazeri* leaf, use chervil or baby celery leaves as a substitute.

METHOD

Prepare *ayu* mousse. Preheat oven to 180°C (350°F). Rub *ayu* bones and head with some oil and salt. Roast until golden brown. Process into a powder.

Whisk egg whites until stiff peaks. Process *ayu* fillet with pork fat and ice cubes to obtain a fine mousse. Mix in whisked egg whites and *ayu* bone powder by hand. Season with salt. Spread *ayu* mousse onto deboned *ayu* and roll into a cylinder. Steam at 85°C (185°F) for a few minutes before grilling over a charcoal grill until fragrant. Set aside.

Prepare sake gel. Combine water and agar agar in a bowl. Place 80 g (2⁴/₅ oz) of mixture with sake in a food processor. Set aside.

Prepare miso cream. Beat egg yolk, grapeseed oil, argan oil and salt until thickened. Season with lemon juice. Mix with miso paste. Rest for 1 hour before using.

Prepare fish fumet. Bring *ayu* bones, kombu and cold water to a boil in a large pot. Lower heat and simmer for 10 minutes. Remove kombu and add baby silver herrings. Cook for 30–40 minutes. Strain stock.

Prepare silver herring paste. Drain silver herrings and pat dry with paper towel. Heat 1 Tbsp oil in a pan over medium heat. Sauté silver herrings until fragrant and golden brown. Drain excess oil. Combine with fish fumet and squid ink in a food processor to obtain a paste. Set aside.

Prepare *yamazeri* purée. Bring water to a boil in a large heatproof bowl. Add salt. Place *yamazeri* leaves and salted water in a food processor to obtain a smooth purée.

Slice grilled *ayu* and arrange on serving plates. Drizzle with *yamazeri* purée, and serve with sake gel and silver herring paste. Garnish as desired.

MARGARITA FORÉS

Owner and
Executive Chef, CIBO

Manila, Philippines

Modern Filipino cuisine

Cooking style.
Modern Filipino.

Background story behind this dish
What I love about this dish is that it perfectly represents my Italian culinary background and how I eventually came to appreciate my national cuisine.

Biggest misconception about Filipino cuisine
It's not all about the exotic stuff like *balut* and adobo and our food being very brown, which is often mentioned in the press. There should be a stronger focus on places where our local cuisine is executed correctly and with the best ingredients.

Biggest achievement
The wave of recognition on the international stage – from presenting Filipino cuisine at Madrid Fusion as well as helping bring Madrid Fusion to Manila, presenting in Identita Golose in Milan, and most especially, being chosen as Asia's Best Female Chef 2016. It's a validation of the work that I've done for the past 30 years.

Cooking tips
The chef who aspires to succeed should be like a sponge. They should learn as much as they can from their home town and culture, and have a desire to travel around their country as well as around the world. The learning and inspiration they gain from their travels, experiences, and from meeting other people in the industry, will help set a chef apart.

Crab Milhojas of Water Spinach Gnocco and Calamondin Gel

Serves 2–4

CRAB MEAT

4 crabs, 50 g (1³/₄ oz) fat extracted, then cooked and meat picked

CALAMONDIN GEL

80 ml (2⁴/₅ fl oz / ⁴/₅ cup) calamondin juice

1 tsp xanthan gum

20 ml (³/₅ fl oz) water

5 g (¹/₆ oz) sugar

CRAB FAT MOUSSE

150 ml (5 fl oz / ³/₅ cup) cooking cream

50 g (1³/₄ oz) crab fat

2 g rock salt

1 g xanthan gum

MUSCOVADO TUBA GLAZE

50 g (1³/₄ oz) muscovado sugar

80 ml (2⁴/₅ fl oz / ⁴/₅ cup) *sukang tuba* (coconut nectar vinegar)

SPINACH GNOCCO

75 g (2³/₅ oz) spinach, blanched

120 ml (4 fl oz / ¹/₂ cup) water

500 g (1 lb 1¹/₂ oz) all-purpose flour

10 g (¹/₃ oz) lard

8 g (¹/₃ oz) salt

20 g (²/₃ oz) sugar

¹/₂ egg

2 Tbsp olive oil

Oil for deep-frying

METHOD

Prepare calamondin gel 4 hours ahead. Combine all ingredients in a food processor and process until thick and smooth. Transfer to a container. Set aside for 4 hours for the air to be released.

Prepare crab fat mousse. Place all ingredients in a food processor and process until thick and smooth. Set aside.

Prepare muscovado tuba glaze. Combine muscovado sugar and *sukang* tuba in a saucepan over medium heat until sugar dissolves. Set aside to cool.

Prepare spinach *gnocco*. Combine blanched spinach and water in a food processor and process into a purée.

Place flour onto a working surface and create a small well. Place lard in the centre of the well, then add all the other ingredients. With clean hands, mix everything together and work dough for 10 minutes. Once dough is ready, place in a container and cover with a kitchen cloth or cling wrap. Let rest for 30 minutes.

Flatten dough into a thick disc between your hands and place through a pasta machine set to the widest setting. Run dough through roller a few times to flatten until you reach 5 mm thickness. Cut into 2.5 × 7.5-cm (1 x 3-in) pieces.

Heat sufficient oil for deep-frying in a pan. Deep-fry spinach *gnocco* until crisp but not brown.

Layer spinach *gnocco* with crab meat, calamondin gel, crab fat mousse and muscovado tuba glaze. Serve.

RENU HOMSOMBAT

Head Chef, SAFFRON

Bangkok, Thailand

Thai cuisine

Cooking style
Authentic Thai flavours with an innovative twist.

Cooking philosophy
Love what you do, and do the best with what you love.

Motivation to becoming a chef
I fell in love with cooking ever since I was a young child. My mother cooked all the time and I was really inspired by how her dishes made everyone so happy.

Favourite ingredients
Thai herbs such as galangal, lemongrass, kaffir lime leaf, basil, and also Thai fruits such as mango and pomelo.

Favourite dish
Stir-fried chicken with chilli and basil.

Kitchen utensil you can't live without
Definitely my chef knife and mortar and pestle because some Thai ingredients need to be peeled, sliced, chopped and pounded to prepare curry paste.

Cooking tips
Pay attention to every detail of the cooking process and use good quality ingredients. If you're looking for inspiration, take a trip to the local markets and look for seasonal ingredients that can be incorporated into your dishes. It is also very important for chefs to cook from their hearts.

Yum Pla Salmon

Serves 2–4

1 Tbsp vegetable oil

250 g (9 oz) fresh salmon, sliced

$^1/_2$ tsp salt

$^1/_2$ tsp ground white pepper

1 tsp finely chopped bird's eye chillies

2 tsp finely chopped garlic

2 tsp finely chopped coriander roots

$^1/_2$ tsp dried chilli flakes

35 g (1$^1/_5$ oz) pomelo sacs

8 g ($^1/_3$ oz) mint leaves

17 g ($^3/_5$ oz) shallots, peeled and finely sliced

17 g ($^3/_5$ oz) crispy pork squares

YUM DRESSING

4 Tbsp fish sauce

6 Tbsp lime juice

2 Tbsp palm sugar

GARNISH

Basil

Coriander leaves

1 large red chilli, cut into strips

NOTE
Yum pla salmon refers to grilled salmon salad.

METHOD

Heat a pan over medium heat. Add a small amount of oil, ensuring that surface of pan is fully coated. Once oil is hot, add salmon and sprinkle with salt and pepper. Allow salmon to cook for 4 minutes on each side. Remove from heat. Set aside.

Prepare *yum* dressing. Combine ingredients for *yum* dressing in a medium bowl. Add chopped bird's eyes chillies, garlic, coriander roots and dried chilli flakes. Stir all ingredients together. Add salmon, followed by pomelo and mint leaves. Gently toss all ingredients together, being careful not to bruise leaves

Serve salmon salad with crispy pork squares. Garnish as desired.

**SEUNG HWAN
CARLOS SHIN**

Head Chef and
R&D Director, TERRENO

Seoul, South Korea

Spanish cuisine

Cooking style
Natural and authentic.

Motivation to becoming a chef
I wanted to continue the family business started by my grandmother. Every meal my grandmother made was really delicious so I wanted to be a chef who can make dishes that tasted as good as hers.

Cooking philosophy
No use of additives and chemicals. Work with a great interest in the kitchen and be professional.

Favourite ingredient
Salted cod fish from Spain which is called *bacalao*. The flesh of salted cod fish is rich in collagen and useful for making many great sauces.

Best thing about being a chef
To be able to work with and make friends with people from various countries.

Favourite food city
My favourite cuisine is Basque cuisine and my favourite city is San Sebastian in Spain. The quality of ingredients and standard of gastronomy is extremely high and every dish I had there was amazing.

Earliest memory with food
I had traditional Japanese sashimi and sushi with my grandmother in the middle of a bamboo forest in Japan. I do not remember which city it was, but the food was served on small boats floating on the water channel.

Octopus in Jerez Vinegar with Sweet Potato and Smoked Paprika

Serves 2–4

20 ml ($^3/_5$ fl oz) olive oil

2 cloves garlic, peeled and smashed

2 sprigs thyme

2–4 octopus tentacles

A pinch of salt

A pinch of sweet smoked paprika

A pinch of maldon salt

2 Tbsp early harvested extra virgin olive oil

VINAIGRETTE
200 ml ($6^3/_4$ fl oz / $^4/_5$ cup) extra virgin olive oil

$3^1/_2$ Tbsp sherry vinegar

30 g (1 oz) black sugar

A pinch of salt

MASHED SWEET POTATOES
50 g ($1^3/_4$ oz) sweet potatoes, peeled and sliced

30 g (1 oz) butter

100 ml ($3^1/_2$ fl oz / $^2/_5$ cup) milk

TIP
If you do not have a sous vide machine, sear octopus in the pan with garlic and thyme, then bring vinaigrette to a boil in a pan. Let octopus and vinaigrette sit for a day in the chiller and reheat before serving.

METHOD

Prepare vinaigrette. Mix olive oil, sherry vinegar and black sugar in a bowl. Adjust with salt to taste. Set aside.

Heat oil in a pan over medium heat. Add garlic, thyme and octopus tentacles. Remove from heat.

Place octopus tentacles and vinaigrette in a vacuum bag. Submerge bag in 72°C (161°F) water for 2 hours.

Prepare mashed sweet potatoes. Heat potatoes with butter and milk in a small saucepan over medium heat. Cook until potatoes are soft. Remove from heat and mash with a hand-held blender.

Arrange cooked octopus and mashed sweet potatoes on a serving plate and sprinkle with sweet smoked paprika and maldon salt. Drizzle early harvested extra virgin olive over.

SURAKIT KHEMKAEW

Chef, CIELO ROOFTOP SKY BAR AND RESTAURANT

Bangkok, Thailand

Innovative Thai,
Modern Western cuisine

Cooking style
Innovative Thai.

Background story behind this dish
My inspiration behind this dish is a traditional Thai appetiser of dried fish served with fresh watermelon that's enjoyed during the summer or the Thai new year.

Cooking philosophy
A good kitchen depends on the team, but a good team depends on the leader. I am considered the leader of a team. Therefore, my responsibility is to be a good role model for them.

Favourite food
Every cuisine has its own uniqueness and different identity. In my opinion, Thai cuisine has the most charm in terms of taste and variety.

Favourite ingredient
Thai traditional dried fish with its unique smoky flavour and dryness of the fish. Dried fish can be used in many different dishes.

Dried Trout with Watermelon

Serves 2–4

50 g (1³/₄ oz) trout, sliced into small pieces

30 g (1 oz) sliced red onions

Oil as needed

Salt to taste

30 g (1 oz) sugar

50 g (1³/₄ oz) red watermelon

50 g (1³/₄ oz) yellow watermelon

GARNISH
Sugar with dried fish flavour

Watermelon gel

Spinach gel

Pansy flowers

Microgreens

METHOD

Preheat oven to 150°C (300°F). Place trout on a baking tray and bake trout for 10 minutes. Remove trout from oven and process in a food processor to obtain trout floss.

Heat oil in a pan over medium heat. Sauté red onions until golden brown. Remove from heat. Transfer to a plate lined with paper towels. Reserve oil.

Heat a non-stick pan with reserved oil over low-medium heat. Place trout floss into pan and stir in same direction until golden brown and crisp.

Season with salt to taste. Add sugar and cooked red onions and continue to stir in pan for 30 minutes.

Cut watermelon into preferred shapes and sizes and place on a serving plate. Sprinkle with trout floss and garnish with sugar, watermelon gel, spinach gel, pansy flowers and microgreens.

TAKU SEKINE

Co-founder and Chef,
DERSOU

Paris, France

Freestyle French cuisine

Cooking style
International freestyle.

Background story behind this dish
This dish is a perfect representation of the cuisine I prepare. I like to work with good ingredients and present them in a simple manner.

Dreams and aspirations
Opening an auberge next to the sea where we have everything – food, sun, beach and life.

Favourite food city
Tokyo and New York for their diversity and depth.

Most underrated Asian ingredient
All *himono* (Japanese dehydrated fish).

Cooking tips
Get good products from local farmers.

Best thing about being a chef
I can create food that I want to eat.

Favourite memory as a chef
Cooking in a lot of places all over the world.

Biggest misconception about Asian food
That it's cheap and dirty.

Dish you would make with a jar of soy sauce
Lu rou fan (Taiwanese braised pork rice) sauce.

Scallops with Apple and Kombawa

Serves 1

4 scallops

Extra virgin olive oil to taste

Fleur de sel to taste

Lime zest to taste

Lime juice to taste

Kombawa (kaffir lime) zest to taste

Fresh horseradish to taste

APPLE JELLY

2 apples, seeded and cut into quarters

8 g (1/3 oz) gelatin, soaked in iced water

GARNISH

Dill

Rucola

Flowers

METHOD

Open scallops and clean with a little bit of water to remove sand. Cut into slices.

Prepare apple jelly. Place apples in a cold press machine to obtain juice. Squeeze out excess water from gelatin. Heat apple juice over low heat and add gelatin. Stir until gelatin is dissolved. Set aside to cool in refrigerator.

Arrange sliced scallops on a serving plate and season with olive oil, fleur de sel, lime zest, lime juice, *kombawa* zest and fresh horseradish.

Top with apple jelly. Garnish with dill, rucola and flowers.

**WUTTISAK
WUTTIAMPORN**

Chef, ETHO'S
RESTAURANT
AND LOUNGE

Phuket, Thailand

Progressive Thai cuisine

Cooking style
Simply elegant.

Main inspiration
Chef René Redzepi, a Danish chef and co-owner of the Michelin 2-starred restaurant Noma in the Christianshavn neighbourhood of Copenhagen, Denmark.

Cooking philosophy
In the kitchen, for everything you create, you need to be aware that the team has to be able to deliver it. Your creative design and decoration is not just for you, but for your staff to be able to follow it as well.

Favourite ingredient
Seafood.

Go-to food after a busy dinner service
I enjoy eating a simple plate of fried rice or just cup noodles.

Cooking tips
Forget about trying to create a superb cooking style. It is important for a beginner cook to be able to focus on the task at hand.

Marinated Salmon with Kaffir Lime Leaves

Serves 2–4

100 g (3½ oz) fresh salmon, sliced

KAFFIR LIME DRESSING
50 g (1¾ oz) kaffir lime leaves, chopped

Zest from 2 oranges

Juice from 1 orange

1 tsp red wine vinegar

1 tsp olive oil

½ tsp sesame oil

Salt to taste

Ground black pepper to taste

METHOD

Prepare kaffir lime dressing. Combine kaffir lime leaves with orange zest and juice, vinegar and oils. Season with salt and black pepper to taste.

Carefully separate salmon slices, then place in a mixing bowl. Drizzle kaffir lime dressing over and gently toss using your hands. Let salmon marinate for 5–10 minutes.

Place salmon on a serving plate. Pour any leftover dressing over. Garnish as desired.

VICKY LAU

**Owner and Head Chef,
TATE DINING ROOM
AND BAR**

Hong Kong

Innovative cuisine

Cooking style
Detailed with lots of storytelling.

Background story behind this dish
It's a great summer dish with flavours from the sea.

Cooking philosophy
Pay attention to seasons and always use the best ingredients available. What you put into a dish is just as important as what you leave out. Be playful and cook for yourself to make yourself happy.

Favourite food city
Tokyo. It is one of the best places to find fresh produce.

Favourite memory as a chef
The first dinner service held at Tate. I invited all of my closest friends and family. I was so nervous my hands were shaking the whole time.

Botan Ebi in Shrimp and Lemongrass Consommé with Ostera Schrencki Caviar and Bafun Uni

Serves 8

10 g (¹/₃ oz) *bafun uni*
(sea urchin)

30 g (1 oz) *ostera schrencki* caviar

SHRIMP AND LEMONGRASS CONSOMMÉ

500 g (1 lb 1¹/₂ oz) shrimps

¹/₂ stalk lemongrass

3 g (¹/₁₀ oz) ginger, peeled

1 tomato

1 clove garlic, peeled

1 g *kampot* peppercorns

¹/₂ bird's eye chilli (optional)

350 ml (11²/₃ fl oz / 1¹/₂ cups)
distilled water

1 tsp fish sauce

BOTAN EBI

8 *botan ebi* (sweet raw shrimps),
washed, peeled and deveined

Light soy sauce to taste

Ground white pepper to taste

Grated lime zest to taste

2 g chives, chopped

METHOD

Prepare shrimp and lemongrass consommé. Combine shrimps, lemongrass, ginger, tomato, garlic, *kampot* peppercorns, bird's eye chilli and distilled water in a food processor and process until mixture is smooth.

Transfer mixture to a heavy-bottomed stockpot and simmer over medium heat for 45 minutes without bringing to a boil. Stir constantly with a spatula until mixture starts to simmer. Remove pot from heat. Gently scoop out mixture and strain through a fine cheese cloth. Season with fish sauce.

Prepare *botan ebi*. Rinse *botan ebi* thoroughly in iced water. Pat dry and cut into small pieces. Season with soy sauce, pepper, grated lime zest and chopped chives. Mix gently with a rubber spatula.

Place a ring mould in the centre of each serving bowl. Fill mould with a spoonful of *botan ebi* and top with a layer a of caviar. Remove ring mould slowly. Garnish with *bafun uni*.

Slowly pour shrimp and lemongrass consommé into the side of bowls. Serve immediately.

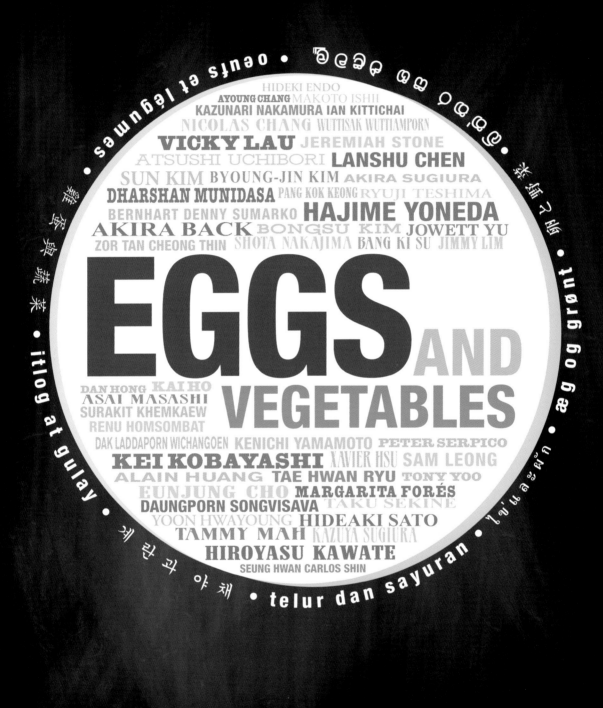

Atsushi Uchibori
MUSHROOM-STUFFED POTATO WITH PORCINI SAUCE | 86

Ian Kittichai
BANANA BLOSSOM AND HEART OF PALM SALAD IN CHILLI JAM DRESSING | 88

Kazunari Nakamura
ROASTED SHIITAKE MUSHROOMS WITH ONION GRATIN AND YUZU MISO | 90

Kei Kobayashi
GARDEN OF VEGETABLES WITH FOAM OF ROCKET AND ANCHOVY MAYONNAISE | 92

Makoto Ishii
MUSHROOM SABLÉ | 94

Nicolas Chang
ROASTED ASPARAGUS, CHAYOTE WITH BLACK GARLIC AND MULLET ROE | 96

Shota Nakajima
ONSEN TAMAGO FU | 98

Zor Tan Cheong Thin
SWEET POTATO WITH SALTED EGG YOLK AND BUCKWHEAT PUFF | 100

ATSUSHI UCHIBORI

Chef, EBURIKO

Karuizawa, Japan

French cuisine (specialising
in mushrooms)

Cooking style
I love to cook mushrooms with French
techniques.

Biggest achievement
Introducing the appeal of mushrooms to
many people. I would like to continue
doing so.

Dreams and aspirations
I want to expand on the potential of
mushrooms and create new recipes.

Cooking philosophy
Respect the ingredient and maximise its
potential.

Kitchen utensil you can't live without
Salamandre.

Go-to food after a busy dinner service
Mizutaki (chicken hot pot).

Cooking tips
Enjoy the cooking and observe the process.

Mushroom-stuffed Potato with Porcini Sauce

Serves 4

Oil as needed

100 g (3¹/₂ oz) mushrooms of your
choice, diced

4 medium potatoes

2 Tbsp fresh cream

Salt to taste

Ground black pepper to taste

STEWED BEEF CHEEKS

500 g (1 lb 1¹/₂ oz) beef cheeks

300 ml (10 fl oz / 1¹/₄ cups)
red wine

100 ml (3¹/₂ fl oz / ²/₅ cup) bouillon

PORCINI POWDER

5 dried porcini mushrooms

PURÉED PORCINI

100 g (3¹/₂ oz) porcini mushrooms,
cut into 1-cm (¹/₂-in) pieces

100 ml (3¹/₂ fl oz / ²/₅ cup) bouillon

2 Tbsp fresh cream

10 g (¹/₃ oz) butter

METHOD

Prepare stewed beef cheeks. Place beef cheeks in a heavy-bottomed pan with red wine and bouillon and simmer over low heat for 3 hours. Remove beef cheeks and cook sauce until reduced. Reserve sauce for later. Set beef cheeks aside to cool before dicing into 7–8 mm ($^1/_5$-in) pieces.

Prepare porcini powder. Place dried porcini mushrooms in a food processor and process until fine. Set aside.

Prepare puréed porcini. Place porcini mushrooms and bouillon in a pot and bring to a boil. Add fresh cream and butter and cook until mushrooms are soft. Place mushrooms in a food processor and process into a purée.

Heat oil in a pan over medium heat. Sauté mushrooms. Remove from heat. Set aside.

Preheat oven to 180°C (350°F).

Bring potatoes in a pot to a boil. Ensure that potatoes remain firm. Remove from heat and set aside to cool. Peel potatoes then mash roughly with fresh cream. Season with salt and pepper. Add diced stewed beef cheeks and diced mushrooms. Mix well. Divide into 4 balls and place on a baking tray. Bake for 10 minutes.

To serve, spoon some stewed beef cheek sauce on a serving plate, and arrange a potato beef ball in the centre. Top with puréed porcini and sprinkle with porcini powder. Garnish as desired.

IAN KITTICHAI

Owner and Chef,
ISSAYA SIAMESE CLUB

Bangkok, Thailand

Thai cuisine

Cooking style
Ingredient-driven.

Main inspiration
My mother. She had a green grocery and a food cart in Bangkok and worked 365 days a year to support my seven sisters and I.

Cooking philosophy
Cook with the best possible ingredients. Keep it simple and keep it fresh.

Favourite ingredient
Fish – it seems so simple, but it is a challenge to clean, cut and cook fish perfectly.

Most underrated Asian ingredient
Kaffir lime leaves.

Most overrated Asian ingredient
Sriracha sauce.

Banana Blossom and Heart of Palm Salad in Chilli Jam Dressing

Serves 4

2 Tbsp lime juice

1 litre (32 fl oz / 4 cups) cold water

DRESSING

500 ml (16 fl oz / 2 cups) tamarind juice

3¹/₂ Tbsp coconut cream

40 g (1¹/₃ oz) palm sugar

100 g (3¹/₂ oz) chilli jam (roasted chilli paste in oil)

1 Tbsp light soy sauce

TURMERIC CREAM

110 ml (3⁴/₅ fl oz / ¹/₂ cup) coconut cream

5 g (¹/₆ oz) turmeric powder

5 g (¹/₆ oz) cornflour

SALAD

100 g (3¹/₂ oz) banana blossoms

50 g (1³/₄ oz) heart of palm, diced into 2-cm (³/₄-in) pieces

30 g (1 oz) deep-fried shallots, thinly sliced

30 g (1 oz) toasted shredded coconut or toasted coconut flakes

5 g (¹/₆ oz) dried chilli flakes

30 g (1 oz) roasted peanuts, chopped

2 kaffir lime leaves, veins removed and finely chopped

GARNISH

1 butterfly pea flower, shredded (optional)

5 g (¹/₆ oz) Chinese broccoli flowers (optional)

2 g red chillies, seeded and julienned

2 kaffir lime leaves, veins removed and finely chopped

METHOD

Prepare dressing. Combine all ingredients in a pot and bring to a boil. Remove from heat. Set aside.

Prepare turmeric cream. Combine all ingredients in a saucepan and bring to a boil until a thick consistency is obtained, stirring constantly. Set aside.

Add lime juice to a bath of cold water.

Prepare banana blossoms for salad. Peel away and discard outer red petals of banana blossom. Remove small white strips of banana flower along with them. Cut off the tip at the end of the blossom. Split the blossom into half lengthwise, then cut the pieces into half again to obtain a quartered blossom.

Place into a water bath to prevent the blossoms from oxidising. Proceed to peel and clean each layer of the blossom, making sure to discard the small white strips of banana flower inside.

Dice cleaned blossoms into 2-cm ($^3/_4$-in) squares and return the pieces to the water bath as you continue to chop the rest. Once finished, drain excess water.

Prepare salad. Heat banana blossom and heart of palm in a pan with dressing until warm. Remove from heat. Toss in deep-fried shallots, toasted coconut, chilli flakes, roasted peanuts and 2 kaffir lime leaves, and mix together.

Transfer to a serving plate. Drizzle turmeric cream over and garnish with assorted flowers, red chillies and kaffir lime leaves.

Dreams and aspirations for the future
I want to enhance the restaurant's standing in Japan.

Cooking philosophy
Farm to table.

Best thing about being a chef
I can eat delicious food every day.

Earliest memory with food
Milkshake.

First recipe you ever made
A simple sandwich.

KAZUNARI NAKAMURA

Chef, LA BONNE TABLE

Tokyo, Japan

French cuisine

Roasted Shiitake Mushrooms with Onion Gratin and Yuzu Miso

Serves 4

4 fresh shiitake mushrooms, stems removed

12 g (¹/₂ oz) walnuts

YUZU MISO
100 g (3¹/₂ oz) yuzu peel
100 g (3¹/₂ oz) miso

ONION GRATIN
1 Tbsp butter
3 onions, peeled and sliced

METHOD

Preheat oven to 220°C (440°F).

Prepare yuzu miso. Combine yuzu peel and miso in a food processor and process into a paste. Set aside.

Prepare onion gratin. Heat butter in a pan over medium heat. Sauté sliced onions for 30 minutes. Remove from heat and set aside.

Roast mushrooms in oven for 3 minutes.

Place 1 tsp onion gratin, 3 g walnuts and 1 g yuzu miso in the cavity of each mushroom. Roast for another 3 minutes.

Serve.

KEI KOBAYASHI

Owner and Chef,
RESTAURANT KEI

Paris, France

French Gastronomy cuisine

Cooking style

My style of cuisine is unique. I am a Japanese chef making French haute cuisine. In my cuisine, you will find influence from Japan (aesthetics, exactness, harmony of colours and delicacy of flavours) and you will recognise the heritage of the classic French recipes.

Background story behind this dish

This is my signature dish that is served at Restaurant Kei. The recipe changes all year long depending on the availability of the vegetables. I really love this dish because of the different vegetables in it. This dish is like a surprise as you never know what you might get.

Main motivation to becoming a chef

When I was 15, I saw a TV show featuring Chef Alain Chapel, a famous French chef, and I knew I wanted to be a chef in France. After some experience in Japan in French restaurants, I went to France in my early 20s to learn French cuisine. It was very important for me to learn about the French regions of specialty and apply them to my Japanese background to create my own cuisine.

First recipe you ever made

The first recipe I ever created is lacquered pigeon with miso condiment. It is a dish you can still find in my restaurant. I like this recipe because it is a mix of both my heart countries: France with the pigeon and Japan with the miso.

Garden of Vegetables with Foam of Rocket and Anchovy Mayonnaise

Serves 10

120 g (4²/₃ oz) smoked salmon

Fleur de sel as needed

A dash of olive oil

Basil oil as needed

VEGETABLE SALAD

Round zucchini, washed and sliced

Zephyr zucchini, washed and sliced

Gold Rush zucchini, washed and sliced

Multi-coloured radishes, washed and sliced

Multi-coloured carrots, washed and sliced

Beetroot, washed and sliced

Runner beans, washed and sliced

ROCKET MASH (FOR ROCKET FOAM)

2 bunches basil, leaves removed from stalk

500 g (1 lb 1½ oz) rocket, washed

Olive oil as needed

1 clove garlic, peeled

ROCKET FOAM

200 g (7 oz) rocket mash

200 ml (6³/₄ fl oz / ⁴/₅ cup) full cream

250 ml (8 fl oz / 1 cup) yoghurt

Salt to taste

Sugar to taste

OLIVE SAUCE

500 g (1 lb 1½ oz) pitted black olives

160 ml (5¹/₃ fl oz / ³/₅ cup) olive oil

2 tsp caper juice

80 g (2⁴/₅ oz) capers

4 Tbsp water

2 cloves garlic, peeled and sliced

ANCHOVY MASH

100 g (3¹/₂ oz) salted anchovies

100 ml (3¹/₂ fl oz / ²/₅ cup) milk

ANCHOVY MAYONNAISE

1 egg, egg yolk and egg white separated

250 ml (8 fl oz / 1 cup) grapeseed oil

2 Tbsp anchovy mash

2 tsp Dijon mustard

Juice from ¹/₂ lemon

Sugar to taste

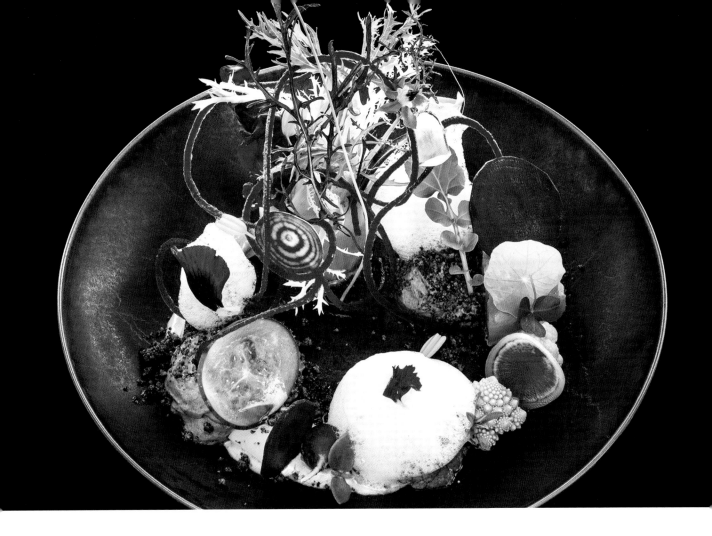

METHOD

Prepare rocket mash. Place basil leaves and rocket in a pan and sweat with olive oil. Prick garlic with a fork. Add to pan and mix well. Remove from heat and set aside to cool. Mix and whisk with more olive oil until soft and mushy. Pass rocket mash through a sieve.

Prepare rocket foam. Mix rocket mash with other ingredients. Place into a *espuma* gun. Keep refrigerated.

Prepare olive sauce. Mix all ingredients together for 5 minutes in a bowl, then process in a mortar and pestle or a food processor until sauce is obtained. Set aside.

Prepare anchovy mash. Place anchovies and milk in a food processor. Process for 5 minutes. Place anchovy mash through a sieve.

Prepare anchovy mayonnaise. Mix egg yolk into a medium mixing bowl using a whisk. Allow a small amount of grapeseed oil to drip into the bowl while stirring briskly with whisk. Once the mixture has begun to thicken and increase in volume, slowly pour more oil in. Continue to vigorously stir in remaining oil. Season with remaining ingredients and olive sauce. Keep refrigerated.

Place anchovy mash and anchovy mayonnaise on a serving plate, then arrange vegetable salad over the mash and mayonnaise. Top with a piece of smoked salmon. Season with fleur de sel and a dash of olive oil. Squeeze rocket foam onto plate. Drizzle with basil oil. Garnish as desired.

MAKOTO ISHII

Owner and Head Chef,
LE MUSÉE

Hokkaido, Japan

French Gastronomy cuisine

Cooking style
Clarity and fantasy.

Main inspiration
Michel Bras of Laguiole, France. He has created culinary miracles out of nothing more than the nature indigenous to his local region.

Motivation to becoming a chef
I've been cooking my own dishes ever since I was a little boy, and I always felt it was my mission in life.

Cooking philosophy
I always try to keep my focus and stay open to new possibilities and potentialities that may arise at any moment in the process of cooking. Spontaneity is the key to creativity.

Kitchen utensil you can't live without
My set of kitchen knives.

Cooking tips
It's all about being prepared.

Mushroom Sablé

Serves 2–4

60 g (2 oz) all-purpose flour

25 g (⁴/₅ oz) almond powder

25 g (⁴/₅ oz) shiitake mushroom powder

10 g (¹/₃ oz) cornstarch

20 g (²/₃ oz) powdered sugar

5 g (¹/₆ oz) salt

150 g (5¹/₃ oz) unsalted butter, cut into cubes

Truffles (optional)

METHOD

Preheat oven to 150°C (300°F).

Combine all ingredients except for butter and truffles in a mixing bowl and pass them through a sieve.

Place butter on top of powdered mixture. Using your hands, work mixture into the butter. Continue rubbing until dough is obtained. Set dough aside to chill in refrigerator.

Divide chilled dough into 5 g (¹/₆ oz) balls and form into discs.

Chill dough discs in refrigerator, then remove and bake in oven at 150°C (300°F) for 13 minutes. Set aside to cool at room temperature.

Top with truffles. Serve.

NICOLAS CHANG

Owner and Head Chef,
RESTAURANT SAVOR

Taipei, Taiwan

Modern French cuisine

Cooking style
Ultra elegant.

Background story behind this dish
This is a dish that was inspired by a trip
to Hualien, Taiwan. The sun was shining
down through the woods and bushes with
shadows in between. I was fascinated by
how the sunlight changed between the
leaves and how it curved. Inspired by the
colour green, I used roasted asparagus and
chayote as the leaves and black garlic to
represent the shadows.

Main inspiration
Nature has always been my source of
inspiration.

Best thing about being a chef
I love being a chef! I love making people
happy, meeting new friends and turning
inspiration into creation. I feel more
connected than ever to the produce, soil,
rocks and ocean, and I love that I am
capable of expressing my thoughts through
a dish using my very own hands.

Earliest memory with food
As a child growing up in South America,
one of the most memorable food I had
was grilled Argentinian beef. The smell
of burning wood, the caramelisation from
the meat and dripping fat has been deeply
imprinted in my memory.

Roasted Asparagus, Chayote with Black Garlic and Mullet Roe

Serves 4

1 spear asparagus, peeled with
bottom 5 cm (2 in) cut off and
discarded

1 chayote

JASMINE VINEGAR

3¹/₂ Tbsp white balsamic vinegar

50 g (1³/₄ oz) fresh jasmine flowers

5 tsp water

70 ml (2²/₅ fl oz / ³/₁₀ cup) olive oil

CURED EGG YOLK

100 g (3¹/₂ oz) salt

100 g (3¹/₂ oz) sugar

4 egg yolks

BLACK GARLIC STRIPS

100 g (3¹/₂ oz) black garlic, peeled

3¹/₂ Tbsp kombu dashi

BROCCOLI PURÉE

65 g (2³/₁₀ oz) butter

250 g (9 oz) broccoli head,
chopped

1 g baking soda

25 g (⁴/₅ oz) white cheddar cheese

4 tsp heavy cream

Salt to taste

METHOD

Prepare jasmine vinegar 3–4 weeks ahead. Place white balsamic vinegar and
jasmine flowers into a glass jar. Let infuse for 3–4 weeks, then combine water,
infused jasmine vinegar and oil in a squeeze bottle. Cover and shake well to
emulsify for later use.

Prepare cured egg yolk 4 days ahead. Mix salt and sugar in a bowl. Spread
a layer of the mixture on a 1 cm (¹/₂-in) deep flat container. Place egg yolks
evenly over the mixture and cover completely with remaining mixture then
tightly wrap with plastic. Keep chilled in refrigerator for 4 days.

After 4 days, rinse egg yolks under cold water to remove remaining salt. Gently
pat dry with paper towels. Place egg yolks on a rack with tray at the bottom
and dry in the refrigerator for 2 hours.

Prepare a pot of salted water. Blanch asparagus for 3 minutes then plunge into iced water to retain vibrant colour. Char asparagus quickly over a grill. Cut into 4-cm (1¹/₂-in) lengths and set aside.

Cut chayote into 1-cm (¹/₂-in) strips and form a circle. Prepare 4 circles for each serving.

Preheat oven to 50°C (120°F).

Prepare black garlic strips. Place black garlic in a mini blender and blend, adding kombu dashi gradually until a smooth paste is obtained. Spread black garlic paste on a silicon baking sheet to 2-cm (³/₄-in) height then dry in oven at 50°C (120°F) until it becomes a pliable leather-like sheet. Gently peel off from baking sheet and cut into 3-cm (1-in) strips. Prepare 3 strips for each serving.

Prepare broccoli purée. Melt butter in a pressure cooker. Add broccoli and baking soda and mix well. Cover with a lid and turn on high heat to reach full pressure, then turn to low heat to maintain pressure. Cook for approximately 15 minutes, then remove from heat and allow to cool and depressurise. Place broccoli and cheddar cheese in a food processor and process into a smooth purée. Season with salt to taste if needed.

Spoon broccoli purée onto a serving plate, followed by asparagus. Place chayote ring on top, then top with black garlic strips. Drizzle jasmine vinegar over. Shave cured egg yolks on top, then garnish as desired.

SHOTA NAKAJIMA

Owner and Chef,
ADANA KAISEKI

Washington, USA

Kaiseki cuisine

Cooking style
Northwest Kaiseki.

Background story behind this dish
Onsen tamago fu is a classic *tamago* (egg) dish. Originally made in *ryokans* (traditional Japanese inns), or hotels, the dish is also made at *onsens* (Japanese hot springs). It is typically served for breakfast since all that is needed is to place the eggs in the hot spring for an hour, crack them and pour soy dashi on top. My favourite part of an egg is the yolk so I decided to create a dish with just the egg yolk. The egg yolk in this dish has the texture of soft cheese, which makes it even more enjoyable.

Cooking philosophy
Every dish that goes out should be something that you would want to serve to someone you love and care for.

Favourite dish
Dashi. Dashi is the base of Japanese cuisine and comprises three ingredients: kombu kelp, bonito flakes and water. There are basic techniques on how to make dashi, but every chef does it differently. I've been making dashi for a few years, but I still have no idea what the outcome will be like.

Onsen Tamago Fu

Serves 4

4 eggs

Iced water as needed

Salt as needed

400 ml (13$^1/_2$ fl oz / 1$^3/_5$ cups) dashi

4 Tbsp mirin (rice wine)

4 Tbsp light soy sauce

20 g ($^2/_3$ oz) potato starch, mixed with 3$^1/_2$ Tbsp water

GARNISH

White sturgeon caviar

24k gold flakes

METHOD

Cook eggs in a sous vide machine or a temperature-controlled machine at 62.3°C (144°F) for 1 hour.

Place cooked eggs in iced water to prevent eggs from overcooking. Once cooled, carefully remove shell. Separate egg white from egg yolk with a brush.

Cure egg yolks slightly on both sides with salt. Allow egg yolks to air-dry for 2 hours.

Combine dashi, mirin and soy sauce in a bowl. Add potato starch mixture and boil until a silky consistency is obtained.

Allow sauce to cool before pouring over egg yolks. Garnish with white sturgeon caviar and 24k gold flakes.

TIP
If you do not have a sous vide machine, cook the eggs in a controlled water bath at 62.5°C (145°F).

ZOR TAN CHEONG THIN

Sous Chef, RESTAURANT
ANDRE and Creator, RAW

Singapore and Taiwan

French nouvelle cuisine

Cooking style
Eclectic and vibrant.

Background story behind this dish
This recipe demonstrates how simple
ingredients like sweet potato, salted egg
yolk and buckwheat can be transformed
into an elegant dish.

Motivation to becoming a chef
My parents inspired me to become a chef.
They used to run a hawker stall and
I watched how they were always looking
for the freshest ingredients to prepare the
dishes. Those were difficult times, but that
was the only way they could support the
family.

Dreams and aspirations
To have a restaurant of my own where
I will be able to showcase beautiful dishes.

Worst thing about being a chef
Long working hours. However, it gives me
the opportunity to create new dishes and
improve my cooking skills.

Earliest memory with food
Chicken curry cooked by my mother.
Nothing compares to a home-cooked
meal by mum.

Sweet Potato with Salted Egg Yolk and Buckwheat Puff

Serves 2–4

200 g (7 oz) dried buckwheat

2 medium sweet potatoes

Salt as needed

Olive oil as needed

10 salted egg yolks

Oil for deep-frying

50 g (1³⁄₄ oz) butter

METHOD

Prepare buckwheat 1 day ahead. Preheat oven to 60°C (140°F). Place dried buckwheat
in a pot of lightly salted water and simmer until tender. Drain and spread buckwheat
out evenly on a silicon baking sheet. Place in the oven to dehydrate overnight.

Vacuum-seal sweet potatoes with a little salt and olive oil. Cook in a sous vide machine
at 100°C (210°F) until cooked and tender. Remove sweet potatoes and cut into halves.

Steam salted egg yolks for 5 minutes. Leave to cool, then process salted egg yolks
in a food processor until fine.

Heat sufficient oil for deep-frying in a wok until 190°C (370°F). Deep-fry buckwheat
until puffed and golden brown. Drain well and set aside.

Heat butter in a pan over medium heat. Add ground salted egg yolks, stirring
continuously to ensure that yolks do not burn. Add sweet potatoes and cook for
30 seconds. Carefully remove sweet potatoes from heat.

Arrange sweet potatoes on serving plates. Top with buckwheat puff. Garnish as desired.

TIP
If you do not have a
sous vide machine, cook
the sweet potatoes in a
resealable plastic bag in a
pot of boiling water until
tender. Remove the plastic
bag and wrap the sweet
potatoes with aluminium
foil. Bake at 180°C (350°F)
for a few minutes.

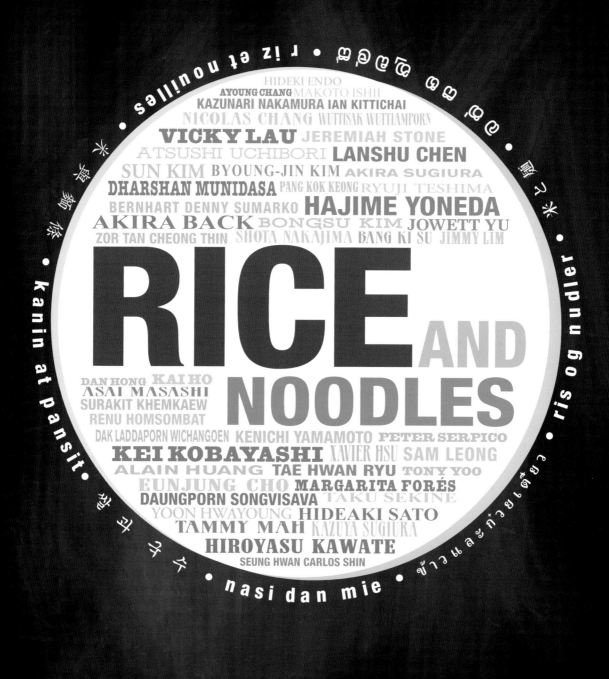

BANG KI SU

Executive Chef, BICENA

Seoul, Korea

Modern Korean cuisine

Cooking style
Fresh and sincere.

Main inspiration
My mother and my mentor Chef Kim Byung Jin. My mother was delicate with her use of Korean sauces and natural ingredients from the mountains. Chef Kim inspired me with his dedication to study ingredients in depth.

Motivation to becoming a chef
I love eating. When I was young, my mother was often busy in the farm so I started making snacks for myself. That became a hobby which turned into a dream.

Cooking philosophy
I don't want my dishes to be just remembered in the mind, I want them to be remembered with feelings and sensations.

Favourite food
Rice. It is symbolic to Korean cuisine.

Best thing about being a chef
Anyone can cook, but only some become chefs. It is extremely difficult to deal with the amount of sacrifice and effort you need to constantly put in when it comes to being a chef. Becoming a chef is a great privilege. Great food can make people happy.

Dried Green Mussel Rice

Serves 2–4

200 g (7 oz) dried daikon greens

Water as needed

2 tsp perilla oil

Salt to taste

300 g (11 oz) mussels

200 g (7 oz) rice, washed and soaked for 30 minutes

METHOD

Soak dried daikon greens in water for 6 hours. Bring to a boil for 2 hours, then wash in cold water. Chop into 5-cm (2-in) lengths.

Heat perilla oil in a pan over medium heat. Add daikon greens and stir-fry lightly. Season with salt to taste.

Boil mussels in a pot with 600 ml (20$^1/_4$ fl oz / 2$^1/_2$ cups) water. Separate shell from meat. Strain stock with a piece of cheesecloth. Measure out 300 ml (10 fl oz / 1$^1/_4$ cups) stock and pour into a ceramic pot.

Drain rice and add to pot of stock. Bring rice and mussels to the boil. Lower heat and cover with a lid for 10 minutes. Simmer for another 3 minutes until rice is done. Spoon daikon greens over cooked rice, cover and set aside. Top with mussels and serve.

PETER SERPICO

Owner and Chef, SERPICO

Philadelphia, USA

American cuisine

Cooking style
Flavour first.

Background story behind this dish
I really enjoy texture in my food and I love that this recipe has lots of texture from the rice cakes and the spring onions.

Worst thing about being a chef
For me, it's the constant criticism. We do our best, but you can't please everyone. I think the longer you deal with it, the less it affects you.

Earliest memory with food
We used to drive from Maryland to Chicago every year for our family vacation. My grandmother would wait for us with an apple pie. It was always served at room temperature and just tasted the best.

Cooking tips
Take your time. Cooking is mostly common sense. If the food doesn't look, smell or sound right, it probably isn't. It takes a long time and a lot of practice to be a good cook.

Korean American Rice Cakes

Serves 4

30 g (1 oz) butter

Sliced spring onions

Toasted white sesame seeds

RICE CAKES

$1^3/_5$ kg ($3^1/_2$ lb) Idaho potatoes

40 g ($1^1/_3$ oz) kosher salt

200 ml ($6^3/_4$ fl oz / $4/_5$ cup) water

$1^1/_2$ kg (3 lb $4^1/_2$ oz) glutinous rice flour

Oil as needed

TIP
Stir-fry rice cakes with some vegetables, and season with soy sauce, chopped ginger and garlic for a healthy and quick lunch.

XO sauce and XO tomato sauce can be stored in an airtight jar and kept refrigerated.

XO SAUCE

$1^1/_{10}$ kg ($2^2/_5$ lb) dried cured ham

6 Chinese sausages

115 g (4 oz) dried shrimps

115 g (4 oz) dried scallops

8 Spanish onions, peeled

4 cloves garlic, peeled

16 dried chillies

230 g (8 oz) ginger, peeled

3.7 litres (125 fl oz / $15^3/_5$ cups) grapeseed oil

115 g (4 oz) paprika

2 sticks Chinese cinnamon

475 ml (16 fl oz / 2 cups) *kochu karu* (Korean red chilli powder)

Zest from 3 oranges

XO TOMATO SAUCE

3 kg ($6^3/_5$ lb) Jersey tomatoes

1 kg (2 lb 3 oz) *gochujang* (Korean chilli paste)

METHOD

Prepare XO sauce 1 day ahead. Soak ham, Chinese sausages, dried shrimps and dried scallops in cold water and leave refrigerated overnight. Drain ingredients and grind on a medium setting in a meat grinder.

Place onions, garlic, chillies and ginger in a food processor and process until fine. Sweat processed ingredients in 1.85 litres (62 fl oz / 7⁴/₅ cups) grapeseed oil until onions are translucent. Add ground meat mixture, remaining oil, paprika, cinnamon and *kochu karu*. Cook over low heat until mixture is dry. Remove from heat and let rest for 1 hour. Set aside to cool completely, then sprinkle with grated orange zest.

Prepare rice cakes. Preheat oven to 170°C (330°F). Poke potatoes with a fork. Roast potatoes for 1¹/₂ hour or until cooked through. Do not undercook potatoes. Let rest for 30 minutes before peeling potatoes and cutting into halves. Pass skinned potatoes through a food mill.

Place milled potatoes and salt in a stand mixer attached with a dough hook. Beat potatoes and gradually add water and glutinous rice flour until incorporated. Roll out into logs and cut into desired size and shape. Bring rice cakes in a pot to a boil. Cook rice cakes until they float to the surface. Remove from heat. Toss rice cakes in oil, then set aside to cool in refrigerator.

Heat oil in a pan over high heat. Stir-fry rice cakes until golden brown on both sides.

Prepare XO tomato sauce. Place tomatoes in a food processor and process until smooth . Add *gochujang* and 2.8 kg (6¹/₁₀ lb) XO sauce. Simmer in a pan for 1 hour over very low heat.

Heat 85 g (3 oz) XO tomato sauce with butter in a pan over low heat. Toss crispy rice cakes in sauce.

Serve with sliced spring onions and toasted white sesame seeds.

SUN KIM

Head Chef, META

Singapore

Contemporary Asian
cuisine

Cooking style
Balanced with lots of flavour.

Background story behind this dish
It's my favourite childhood noodle dish,
and it is easy for home-cooks. I hope that
more people will try my version of *guksu*.

Motivation to becoming a chef
Since young, I have always been curious
about food especially when I was helping
out in my mother's restaurant. It made me
happy to see my family enjoy my cooking.
That was when I realised being a chef was
the right path for me.

Best thing about being a chef
Being able to experiment with different
ingredients and bringing joy and surprise to
my diners as they taste the dishes.

Favourite ingredient
Doenjang (Korean bean paste). It's a
comforting flavour that I grew up with
and I enjoy its subtle umami flavour.

Cooking tips
Understand the ingredients you are using
and be sensitive to the temperature of the
food you are cooking.

Guksu

Serves 4–5

DASHI

500 ml (16 fl oz / 2 cups) water

50 g (1³/₄ oz) anchovies

1 kombu

GUKSU

8 sheets Korean dried seaweed,
soaked in water for 45 minutes
and strained

2 tsp olive oil

4 cloves garlic, peeled and sliced

100 g (3¹/₂ oz) Korean dried
seasoned seaweed

1 tsp yuzu *kosho*

70 g (2¹/₂ oz) capellini pasta

Salt to taste

Ground black pepper to taste

30 g (1 oz) spanner crab meat

GARNISH

20 g (²/₃ oz) chives, finely chopped

30 g (1 oz) yellow zucchini, peeled
and thinly sliced

NOTE

Yuzu *kosho* is a type of
Japanese seasoning usually
made from chilli, yuzu zest
and salt.

TIP

Make sure not to overcook the
pasta. It is important to retain
the texture of the noodles.

METHOD

Prepare dashi. Bring water in a pot to a boil. Add anchovies and kombu and
simmer for 25 minutes. Strain and set aside.

Prepare *guksu*. Cut Korean seaweed into bite-sized pieces. Heat oil in a pot
over medium heat and sauté garlic until golden brown. Add dried seaweed
and seasoned seaweed, and continue to sauté. Add dashi and yuzu *kosho* and
simmer over medium heat for 15 minutes.

In another pot, cook pasta in lightly salted water for 3 minutes. Strain pasta and
add to simmering dashi. Cook for another 2 minutes or until pasta is al dente.

Heat oil in a non-stick frying pan over high heat. Sauté crab meat until fragrant.

Drain and divide pasta into 4–5 servings. Twirl each serving into a tight ball and
arrange on serving plates. Season with salt and pepper. Garnish with chopped
chives, sautéed crab and zucchini.

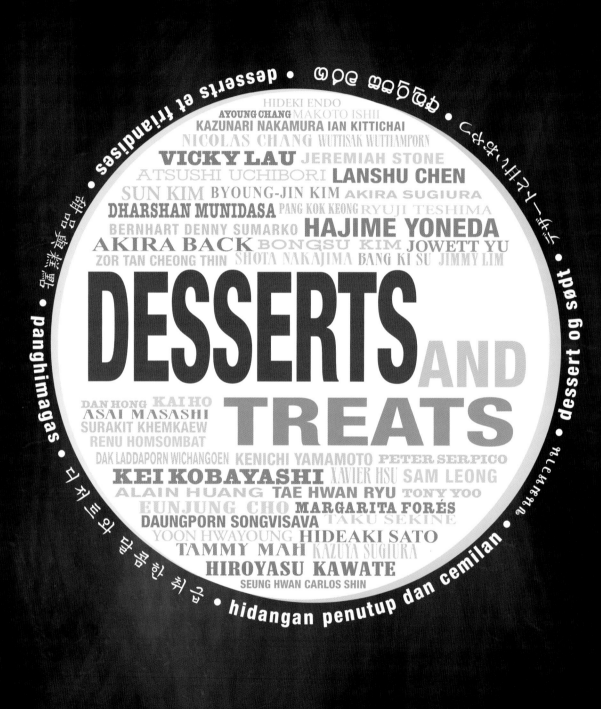

DESSERTS AND TREATS

desserts et friandises

HIDEKI ENDO
AYOUNG CHANG MAKOTO ISHII
KAZUNARI NAKAMURA IAN KITTICHAI
NICOLAS CHANG WUTTISAK WUTTHAMPORN
VICKY LAU JEREMIAH STONE
ATSUSHI UCHIBORI LANSHU CHEN
SUN KIM BYOUNG-JIN KIM AKIRA SUGIURA
DHARSHAN MUNIDASA PANG KOK KEONG RYUJI TESHIMA
BERNHART DENNY SUMARKO HAJIME YONEDA
AKIRA BACK BONGSU KIM JOWETT YU
ZOR TAN CHEONG THIN SHOTA NAKAJIMA BANG KI SU JIMMY LIM

DAN HONG KAI HO
ASAI MASASHI
SURAKIT KHEMKAEW
RENU HOMSOMBAT
DAK LADDAPORN WICHANGOEN KENICHI YAMAMOTO PETER SERPICO
KEI KOBAYASHI XAVIER HSU SAM LEONG
ALAIN HUANG TAE HWAN RYU TONY YOO
EUNJUNG CHO MARGARITA FORÉS
DAUNGPORN SONGVISAVA TAKU SEKINE
YOON HWAYOUNG HIDEAKI SATO
TAMMY MAH KAZUYA SUGIURA
HIROYASU KAWATE
SEUNG HWAN CARLOS SHIN

panghimagas • hidangan penutup dan cemilan • dessert og sødt

EUNJUNG CHO

Owner and Pastry Chef,
HONEYBEE CAKES

Seoul, Korea

Pastry

Cooking style
Sophisticated and delicate.

Baking philosophy
To create desserts and conduct classes with sincerity. I hope that my cakes are an accurate representation of me.

Best thing about being a chef
Sharing my own creations with others. I am happy to see people enjoying my desserts.

Cooking tips
When it comes to baking, it is important that you follow the recipe closely and use the right measurements and ingredients.

Favourite memory as a chef
In 2013, I participated in a campaign which helps kids with life-threatening medical conditions. I invited a pretty little girl to my baking studio and we had a good time making cookies for her friends in the hospital.

Favourite city
Bangkok. I love that they have diverse ingredients that when combined, can make well-balanced dishes.

Ultimate Coffee Chocolate Crunch Bar

Serves 4

COFFEE CHANTILLY
120 ml (4 fl oz / ¹/₂ cup) cream

10 g (¹/₃ oz) ground coffee

12 g (¹/₂ oz) sugar

¹/₂ g gelatin leaves, soaked in cold water for 15–20 minutes

1 g orange peel

CHOCOLATE CHANTILLY
80 ml (2⁴/₅ fl oz / ⁴/₅ cup) cream

30 g (1 oz) milk chocolate

¹/₂ g gelatin leaves, soaked in cold water for 15–20 minutes

HAZELNUT DACQUOISE
65 g (2³/₁₀ oz) egg whites

20 g (²/₃ oz) sugar

55 g (2 oz) hazelnut powder

55 g (2 oz) icing sugar, more as needed

20 g (²/₃ oz) crushed hazelnuts

CHOCOLATE CREAM
80 ml (2⁴/₅ fl oz / ⁴/₅ cup) cream

20 g (²/₃ oz) egg yolks

8 g (¹/₃ oz) sugar

40 g (1¹/₃ oz) dark chocolate

30 g (1 oz) milk chocolate

HAZELNUT CHOCOLATE GLAZE
175 g (6¹/₅ oz) milk chocolate

70 ml (2²/₅ fl oz / ³/₁₀ cup) hazelnut oil

50 g (1³/₄ oz) chopped hazelnuts

NOTE
A *dacquoise* is a dessert consisting of baked layers of nut-flavoured meringue.

METHOD

Prepare coffee and chocolate Chantilly 1 day ahead. For coffee Chantilly, warm cream to 80°C (176°F) and add ground coffee. Mix well for 3 minutes. Strain coffee cream through a sieve. Replenish cream to make up 120 ml (4 fl oz / $^{1}/_{2}$ cup). Stir in sugar, gelatin and orange peel. Refrigerate overnight.

For chocolate Chantilly, warm cream to 80°C (176°F) and add milk chocolate. Mix well until smooth. Stir in gelatin. Refrigerate overnight.

Preheat oven to 175°C (350°F). Line a baking tray. Prepare éclair mould. Set aside.

Prepare hazelnut *dacquoise*. Using a hand mixer, whisk egg whites in a mixing bowl until egg whites start to foam. Add 10 g ($^{1}/_{3}$ oz) sugar. Continue whisking until stiff peaks form. Add remaining sugar and continue to whisk until meringue is smooth and shiny. Add hazelnut powder and icing sugar. Mix well.

Transfer batter to a pastry bag. Pipe batter into éclair shapes similar to the size of the éclair mould on prepared baking tray. Top with crushed hazelnuts and dust with icing sugar. Bake in oven at 175°C (350°F) for 15 minutes. Remove from heat. Set aside to cool completely.

Prepare chocolate cream. Combine cream, egg yolks and sugar in a saucepan. Heat mixture to 80°C (176°F). Add dark chocolate and milk chocolate and mix until smooth. Pour into éclair mould immediately.

Place hazelnut *dacquoise* on chocolate cream. Store in freezer.

Prepare hazelnut chocolate glaze. Melt milk chocolate over low heat. Stir in hazelnut oil and chopped hazelnuts.

Pour hazelnut chocolate glaze onto frozen hazelnut *dacquoise*. Pipe with coffee Chantilly and chocolate Chantilly. Decorate as desired.

HIROYASU KAWATE

Owner and Chef,
FLORILÈGE

Tokyo, Japan

French-Japanese cuisine

Cooking style
French-Japanese.

Background story behind this dish
I've been making Pain D'olive for about six years at Florilège. It was always served to every customer. This dessert is suitable for any occasion, from home parties to buffets.

Biggest achievement
When I received the One to Watch Award for Asia in 2016, at the Asia's 50 Best Restaurants ceremony. I gained many opportunities to cook for overseas visitors because of the award.

Main motivation to becoming a chef
I was influenced by my father because he was a chef. His kitchen was my playground when I was a child.

Earliest memory with food
Hamburger steak which my father made.

Go-to food after a busy dinner service
Soba noodles.

Pain D'olive

Serves 4

280 ml (9¹/₂ fl oz / 1¹/₅ cups) milk

70 ml (2²/₅ fl oz / ³/₁₀ cup) heavy cream (47% fat)

20 g (²/₃ oz) castor sugar

360 g (12³/₅ oz) green olives

5 egg yolks

2 eggs

1 tsp salt

4 squares brioche, cut into 1-cm (¹/₂-in) cubes

Unsalted butter as needed

METHOD

Preheat oven to 200°C (400°F).

Place milk and heavy cream in a heatproof bowl over low heat and warm to 37°C (98.6°F). Add sugar and stir to dissolve.

Combine milk-cream mixture with olives, egg yolks, eggs and salt in a food processor and process until fine. Pass processed ingredients through a sieve.

Using a chopstick, poke a few holes on brioche squares. Pour mixture over brioche and allow brioche to soak in mixture well.

Heat 4 tsp butter in a hot pan over medium heat and toast all surfaces of brioche squares. Place on a baking tray.

Place brioche squares in oven and bake for 5–6 minutes. Remove from heat.

Garnish as desired and serve.

PANG KOK KEONG

Owner and Executive Chef,
ANTOINETTE

Singapore

French Patisserie cuisine

Cooking style
Classical and imaginative.

Background story behind this dish
It is made up of many different elements. What I love about it is that it is visually attractive, filled with many complimentary flavours and has the surprise of smoked nuts in it.

Best thing about being a chef
You get to taste the food first!

Favourite food city
Tokyo. I can stuff my face with great ramen and sushi and they have some of the best patisseries in the world!

Most underrated Asian ingredient
Gula Melaka. Gula Melaka is very much like caramel, only better with hints of coconut and butterscotch.

Cooking tip
Respect traditions.

Favourite memory as a chef
My internship in Spain with Paco Torreblanca.

Terrarium

Makes five 10.5-cm (4-in) semi spheres

30-cm (12-in) square cocoa sponge sheet cake

4 Tbsp dark rum syrup

SMOKED ALMOND NOUGATINE
Wood chips for smoking

75 g (2³/₅ oz) almond strips

5 tsp honey

8 g (¹/₃ oz) glucose

45 g (1¹/₂ oz) butter

1 g pectin

50 g (1³/₄ oz) icing sugar

CARAMELISED BANANAS
70 g (2¹/₂ oz) sugar

15 g (¹/₂ oz) butter

¹/₄ vanilla pod, scraped to obtain seeds

140 g (5 oz) bananas, peeled and sliced

1 Tbsp rum

1 tsp lemon juice

LIGHT PASSION FRUIT CREAM
60 g (2 oz) passion fruit purée

2 gelatin leaves, soaked in water to soften

90 ml (3 fl oz / ³/₈ cup) whipped cream

25 g (⁴/₅ oz) sugar

2 tsp water

20 g (²/₃ oz) egg white

LIGHT CHOCOLATE MOUSSE
48 ml (1³/₅ fl oz / ¹/₅ cup) milk

48 ml (1³/₅ fl oz / ¹/₅ cup) cream

20 g (²/₃ oz) egg yolk

5 g (¹/₆ oz) sugar

145 g (5 oz) Valrhona *manjari* chocolate (64% dark), roughly chopped

240 ml (8 fl oz / 1 cup) whipped cream

METHOD

Prepare smoked almond nougatine. Line a pot with aluminium foil. Place some wood chips in it, then torch chips to create smoke. Place almond strips on a rack over wood chips and cover pot for 20 minutes.

Preheat oven to 160°C (325°F).

Combine honey, glucose and butter in a heatproof bowl. Warm mixture over stove. Mix pectin and icing sugar well and add to honey mixture, stirring gently with each addition. Add smoked almond strips once sugar has dissolved.

Spread mixture on a tray lined with baking paper. Bake for 20 minutes or until evenly browned. Remove and let cool. Store in an airtight container until needed.

Prepare caramelised bananas. Melt sugar in a pot, stirring until sugar caramelises. Add butter and stir to combine. Add vanilla seeds and sliced bananas. Sauté over medium heat, stirring occasionally for 1–2 minutes. Flambé with rum. Remove from heat and add lemon juice. Spread caramelised bananas out on a tray to cool.

Using a 7.5 cm (3 in) ring cutter, cut 5 rounds from cocoa sponge cake. Place caramelised bananas equally over sponge cakes. Drizzle dark rum syrup over. Place in the freezer for at least 3 hours.

Prepare light passion fruit cream. Place one-third passion fruit purée in a large heatproof bowl. Warm up passion fruit purée. Add softened gelatin. Fold in whipped cream and remaining passion fruit purée.

Place sugar in a heavy-bottomed saucepan. Add water. Cook sugar over high heat, stirring only until it comes to a boil.

Using an electric mixer at medium speed, beat egg whites until soft peaks.

Remove sugar syrup from heat. Gradually add to egg whites, beating at low to medium speed. Fold meringue into passion fruit gelatin.

Using an 8.5 cm ($3^2/_5$ in) ring cutter, cut out 5 rounds from cocoa sponge cake. Pipe passion fruit meringue over cakes. Drizzle dark rum syrup over. Place in the freezer for at least 3 hours.

Prepare light chocolate mousse. Combine milk and cream in a medium saucepan and bring to a simmer. Remove from heat.

Using a whisk, whisk egg yolk and sugar in a medium bowl. Gradually whisk hot milk into egg yolk mixture. Return to saucepan. Stir over low heat until custard thickens. Strain over chopped chocolate to achieve an emulsion. Gently fold in whipped cream.

Using the bottom part of a spherical plastic container, pipe a little chocolate mousse at the bottom. Sprinkle large pieces of smoked almond nougatine on mousse. Place a 7.5 cm (3 in) sponge lined with banana over it. Pipe more chocolate mousse over. Place a 8.5 cm ($3^2/_5$ in) sponge lined with passion fruit cream over.

Fill the rest of the space with chocolate mousse. Smooth mousse with the back of a spoon. Using a plain nozzle, pipe a few irregular balls of mousse on the surface. Repeat to make another 4 terrariums. Chill for at least 4 hours before serving.

TAE HWAN RYU

Chef Patron at RYUNIQUE,
NORMAL BY RYUNIQUE

Seoul, Korea

Contemporary cuisine

Cooking style
Hybrid cuisine.

Biggest achievement
My restaurant was awarded the 79th
World's Best Restaurant in 2015. It was
our first award and I simply cannot forget
that day.

Main inspiration
Definitely my father. He loved cooking and
he wanted to be a chef. I strongly believe
that my father influenced my culinary
career.

Earliest memory with food
I spent a long time in Japan, Australia
and the UK training in several famous
restaurants. I lost 20 kg and only had a pair
of jeans and three T-shirts with me. Even
though it was a very hard time for me,
I believe that experience has made me the
chef I am today.

Favourite food city
Japan. I love sushi and I like food with
umami flavours.

Dragonfly

Serves 2–4

DRAGONFLY BODY

100 g (3$^1/_2$ oz) chestnuts

$^1/_4$ bay leaf

$^1/_2$ stem thyme

500 ml (16 fl oz / 2 cups) milk

Salt to taste

DRAGONFLY WINGS

5 pieces kimchi, rinsed

Olive oil as needed

DRAGONFLY TAIL

1 potato, peeled and thinly sliced

DRAGONFLY HEAD

100 g (3$^1/_2$ oz) kimchi sauce

1 g agar agar powder

DRAGONFLY EYES

20 g ($^2/_3$ oz) *gochujang*
(Korean chilli paste)

METHOD

Prepare dragonfly body. Bring all ingredients except salt in a pot to a boil. Remove bay leaf and thyme. Place boiled chestnuts in a food processor to obtain a purée. Push chestnut purée through a sieve. Season with salt. Set aside.

Preheat oven to 63°C (145°F).

Prepare dragonfly wings. Brush kimchi leaves with olive oil. Dehydrate in oven at 63°C (145°F) for 12 hours. Cut leaves to resemble wings of a dragonfly. Prepare 4–8 wings.

Prepare dragonfly tail. Roll potato slices into cylinders and fry until crisp. The tail should be approximately 7 cm (2⁴/₅ in). Prepare 2–4 tails.

Prepare dragonfly head. Place kimchi sauce and agar agar in a pot and bring to a boil. Remove from heat, then place in refrigerator to set. Once set, purée by hand or using a food processor. Place purée through a sieve until fine. Prepare 2–4 heads.

Preheat oven to 160°C (320°F). Prepare dragonfly eyes. Spread *gochujang* out in a thin layer on a baking tray and place in oven to dry roast until slightly soft and chewy in texture. Cut out according to the shape of the eyes of a dragonfly. Prepare 4–8 eyes.

Pipe 8 g (¹/₃ oz) chestnut purée on serving plates for each dragonfly body. Assemble wings, tail, head and eyes.

TAMMY MAH

Executive Pastry Chef,
AMARA HOTELS &
RESORTS, SINGAPORE

Singapore

Pastry

Cooking style
Innovative and surprising.

Background story behind this dish
With the additions of lemongrass and tapioca to the coconut, this dessert is representative of my Peranakan heritage. These ingredients are very common in traditional Peranakan *kueh* (cakes).

Biggest achievement
When I won the WGS Pastry Chef of the Year (People's Choice) award in 2012. It was the first time I felt recognised, and it spurred me on to work even harder.

Main inspiration
My nanny. She piqued my interest with her delicious Peranakan cuisine. When she noticed my growing interest and

fascination with food, she imparted her knowledge and skills to me.

Cooking philosophy
Teamwork makes the dream work; no one gets left behind.

Best thing about being a chef
I can make people from all walks of life expect the unexpected when having my desserts.

First recipe you ever made
Babi pongteh. It is a traditional Peranakan stew consisting of chicken, pork belly, bean paste and several other condiments. I was 10 years old when I first made it. Not only is it my favourite dish, it is also one that remains close to my heart.

Summer Paradise

Serves 2–4

PINEAPPLE SALSA

$^1/_2$ pineapple, core removed, flesh cut into cubes

50 g ($1^3/_4$ oz) sugar

$3^1/_2$ Tbsp sherry vinegar

15 fresh mint leaves

CACAO SOIL

100 g ($3^1/_2$ oz) all-purpose flour

100 g ($3^1/_2$ oz) ground almonds

50 g ($1^3/_4$ oz) brown sugar

50 g ($1^3/_4$ oz) white sugar

100 g ($3^1/_2$ oz) butter

Cocoa powder for coating

COCONUT MOUSSE

150 g ($5^1/_3$ oz) coconut purée

50 g ($1^3/_4$ oz) sugar

5 gelatin leaves, soaked in water to soften

100 g ($3^1/_2$ oz) whipped cream

SAGO

20 g ($^2/_3$ oz) sago pearls

4 Tbsp sugar syrup

NOTE
Peranakans refer to people of mixed Chinese and Malay heritage.

METHOD

Prepare pineapple salsa 1 day ahead. Combine pineapple with sugar, sherry vinegar and mint leaves in a bowl. Marinate overnight. Remove mint leaves the next day.

Prepare cacao soil 1 day ahead. Mix all ingredients except butter and cocoa powder in a mixing bowl.

Cut butter into dry ingredients until pea-sized lumps form loosely. Store in the freezer overnight.

Preheat oven to 170°C (330°F).

Spread cacao soil out on a lined baking tray and bake until golden brown. Toss with an angled palette knife every 15 minutes. Allow crumble to cool before tossing with cocoa powder until evenly coated.

Prepare coconut mousse. Bring coconut purée and sugar in a pot to a boil. Remove pot from heat and add gelatin. Allow mixture to cool until it reaches room temperature. Fold whipped cream into mixture and pipe into desired moulds.

Prepare sago. Boil sago in boiling water until translucent. Rinse under running water. Add cooled sago pearls to sugar syrup and set aside.

Spoon some cacao soil onto serving plates. Top with coconut mousse. Place sago on mousse and top with pineapple salsa.

ABOUT THE
AUTHOR

Michelle Tchea is the founder and owner of Healthy Spoon Pty Ltd, an organics company specialising in innovative Superfoods including Michelle's AUSTRALIAN SuperOats.

Australian-owned and operated, it is headquartered in Melbourne, Australia, and caters to a worldwide audience of conscious eaters.

To fuel her worldly curiosities, Michelle Tchea also manages PopIntel Group, an intelligence strategy firm focused on F&B, with a client base including some of the world's leading luxury hotels, award-winning restaurants and Michelin-starred chefs.

Michelle has been published in *GQ, SCMP, Celebrated Living, Travel+Leisure, Architectural Digest* and other reputable international publications.

Chefs Collective is Michelle's fourth book.

WEIGHTS AND MEASURES

Quantities for this book are given in imperial, metric and American spoon and cup measures. Standard spoon and cup measurements used are: 1 teaspoon = 5 ml, 1 tablespoon = 15 ml. All measures are level unless otherwise stated.

LIQUID AND VOLUME MEASURES

Metric	Imperial	American
5 ml	$1/6$ fl oz	1 teaspoon
10 ml	$1/3$ fl oz	1 dessertspoon
15 ml	$1/2$ fl oz	1 tablespoon
60 ml	2 fl oz	$1/4$ cup (4 tablespoons)
85 ml	$2^1/2$ fl oz	$1/3$ cup
90 ml	3 fl oz	$3/8$ cup (6 tablespoons)
125 ml	4 fl oz	$1/2$ cup
180 ml	6 fl oz	$3/4$ cup
250 ml	8 fl oz	1 cup
300 ml	10 fl oz ($1/2$ pint)	$1^1/4$ cups
375 ml	12 fl oz	$1^1/2$ cups
435 ml	14 fl oz	$1^3/4$ cups
500 ml	16 fl oz	2 cups
625 ml	20 fl oz (1 pint)	$2^1/2$ cups
750 ml	24 fl oz ($1^1/5$ pints)	3 cups
1 litre	32 fl oz ($1^3/5$ pints)	4 cups
1.25 litres	40 fl oz (2 pints)	5 cups
1.5 litres	48 fl oz ($2^2/5$ pints)	6 cups
2.5 litres	80 fl oz (4 pints)	10 cups

OVEN TEMPERATURE

	°C	°F	Gas Regulo
Very slow	120	250	1
Slow	150	300	2
Moderately slow	160	325	3
Moderate	180	350	4
Moderately hot	190/200	370/400	5/6
Hot	210/220	410/440	6/7
Very hot	230	450	8
Super hot	250/290	475/550	9/10

DRY MEASURES

Metric	Imperial
30 grams	1 ounce
45 grams	$1^1/2$ ounces
55 grams	2 ounces
70 grams	$2^1/2$ ounces
85 grams	3 ounces
100 grams	$3^1/2$ ounces
110 grams	4 ounces
125 grams	$4^1/2$ ounces
140 grams	5 ounces
280 grams	10 ounces
450 grams	16 ounces (1 pound)
500 grams	1 pound, $1^1/2$ ounces
700 grams	$1^1/2$ pounds
800 grams	$1^3/4$ pounds
1 kilogram	2 pounds, 3 ounces
1.5 kilograms	3 pounds, $4^1/2$ ounces
2 kilograms	4 pounds, 6 ounces

LENGTH

Metric	Imperial
0.5 cm	$1/4$ inch
1 cm	$1/2$ inch
1.5 cm	$3/4$ inch
2.5 cm	1 inch

ABBREVIATION

tsp	teaspoon
Tbsp	tablespoon
g	gram
kg	kilogram
ml	millilitre

AKIRA BACK ★ AKIRA SUGIURA ★ ALAIN HUANG ★ ASAI MASASHI
MARKO ★ BONGSU KIM ★ BYOUNG-JIN KIM ★ DAK LADDAPORN WICHA
EUNJUNG CHO ★ HAJIME YONEDA ★ HIDEAKI SATO ★ HIDEKI ENDO ★
OWETT YU ★ KAI HO ★ KAZUNARI NAKAMURA ★ KAZUYA SUGIURA ★ K
ARGARITA FORÉS ★ NICOLAS CHANG ★ PANG KOK KEONG ★ PETER S
VAN CARLOS SHIN ★ SHOTA NAKAJIMA ★ SUN KIM ★ SURAKIT KHEMK
U ★ WUTTISAK WUTTIAMPORN ★ XAVIER HSU ★ YOON HWAYOUNG ★ Z
AI MASASHI ★ ATSUSHI UCHIBORI ★ AYOUNG CHANG ★ BANG KI SU ★
DDAPORN WICHANGOEN ★ DAN HONG ★ DAUNGPORN SONGVISAVA
TO ★ HIDEKI ENDO ★ HIROYASU KAWATE ★ IAN KITTICHAI ★ JEREMIA
KAZUYA SUGIURA ★ KEI KOBAYASHI ★ KENICHI YAMAMOTO ★ LANSHU
K KEONG ★ PETER SERPICO ★ RENU HOMSOMBAT ★ RYUJI TESHIMA
M ★ SURAKIT KHEMKAEW ★ TAE HWAN RYU ★ TAKU SEKINE ★ TAMM
U ★ YOON HWAYOUNG ★ ZOR TAN CHEONG THIN ★ AKIRA BACK ★ A
OUNG CHANG ★ BANG KI SU ★ BERNHART DENNY SUMARKO ★ BONGS
AUNGPORN SONGVISAVA ★ DHARSHAN MUNIDASA ★ EUNJUNG CHO
N KITTICHAI ★ JEREMIAH STONE ★ JIMMY LIM ★ JOWETT YU ★ KAI HO
MAMOTO ★ LANSHU CHEN ★ MAKOTO ISHII ★ MARGARITA FORÉS ★ NIC
RYUJI TESHIMA ★ SAM LEONG ★ SEUNG HWAN CARLOS SHIN ★ SHOTA
KINE ★ TAMMY MAH ★ TONY YOO ★ VICKY LAU ★ WUTTISAK WUTTIAM
CK ★ AKIRA SUGIURA ★ ALAIN HUANG ★ ASAI MASASHI ★ ATSUSHI U
BONGSU KIM ★ BYOUNG-JIN KIM ★ DAK LADDAPORN WICHANGOEN
NJUNG CHO ★ HAJIME YONEDA ★ HIDEAKI SATO ★ HIDEKI ENDO ★ H
OWETT YU ★ KAI HO ★ KAZUNARI NAKAMURA ★ KAZUYA SUGIURA ★ K
ARGARITA FORÉS ★ NICOLAS CHANG ★ PANG KOK KEONG ★ PETER S
VAN CARLOS SHIN ★ SHOTA NAKAJIMA ★ SUN KIM ★ SURAKIT KHEMK
U ★ WUTTISAK WUTTIAMPORN ★ XAVIER HSU ★ YOON HWAYOUNG ★ Z
AI MASASHI ★ ATSUSHI UCHIBORI ★ AYOUNG CHANG ★ BANG KI SU
DDAPORN WICHANGOEN ★ DAN HONG ★ DAUNGPORN SONGVISAVA
TO ★ HIDEKI ENDO ★ HIROYASU KAWATE ★ IAN KITTICHAI ★ JEREMIA
KAZUYA SUGIURA ★ KEI KOBAYASHI ★ KENICHI YAMAMOTO ★ LANSHU
K KEONG ★ PETER SERPICO ★ RENU HOMSOMBAT ★ RYUJI TESHIMA